Rethinking Economics:
REFLECTIONS OF AN UNCOMMON ECONOMIST
ESSAYS BY SHELDON STAHL

★ KANSAS CITY STAR BOOKS

Rethinking Economics:
Reflections of an Uncommon Economist
Essays by Sheldon Stahl

EDITOR: Doug Weaver
EDITORIAL ASSISTANCE: John Martellaro
DESIGN: Amy Robertson
COPY EDITING: Judy Pearlstein
PRODUCTION ASSISTANCE: Jo Ann Groves

Published by Kansas City Star Books
1729 Grand Blvd.
Kansas City, Missouri 64108
All rights reserved.
Copyright© 2010 by Sheldon Stahl

No part of this book may be reproduced, stored in a retrieval system, or transmitted in any form or by any means electronic, mechanical, photocopying, recording or otherwise, without the prior consent of the publisher. Permission is granted to make copies of the patterns pages only for your own private, personal use, not for commercial use.

First edition, first printing
ISBN: 978-1-61169-000-2

Printed in the United States.

To order copies, call StarInfo at 816-234-4636 and say "operator."

www.TheKansasCityStore.com

KANSAS CITY STAR BOOKS

*Now, more than ever, our current crises
offer us an opportunity to reach out and to regain
that virtue of humanity that undergirds a civil society.
That task is surely within our reach.*
—SHELDON STAHL

Contents

Foreword 6
Introduction 8
Prologue: Bridging the Divide 11

SECTION I: BEHIND THE NUMBERS
CONNECTING ECONOMICS AND HUMANITY

Behind the Numbers 14
Rethinking Economics 19
On the Virtues of Being Transparent 24
Let's Hear it for the Little Guy 27
On Making a Difference 31
Reaching Too Far? 35
The United Nations at 60: A Balance Sheet 39
On Globalization: The Rest of the Story 42
Through the Efforts of Others 47
Who Wants to Be a Millionare? 51
Putting Your People First: It Makes Dollars and Sense 54
Some Reflections on Avarice and Generosity 56
The Long and the Short of It 61
The Challenge of a Changing Paradigm 63
Labor Day: So What's to Celebrate? 67
Illegal Immigration: We Have Met the Enemy
  and It Is Us. But Who Is Us? 78

SECTION 2: LEARNING FROM HISTORY
ECONOMIC ANALYSIS

The Surprising Economy 88
On Learning From History 94
About That 800 Pound Gorilla 99
Economic Theories 103
The Economy: Is the Glass Half Full or Half Empty? 110

SECTION 3: TALES OF VALUES
REFLECTIONS ON MEANING AND PURPOSE

A Tale of Values 118
Of Old Friends and the Kindness of a Stranger 122
What's in a Word? 127
On Discerning Between Dissent and Disloyalty 131
Embracing Change 135
Managers and Leaders: They're Not the Same 138
On Standing Out in a Crowd 141
Make Your Light Shine 145
On Measuring Success 149
I Wish You Enough 152
In Search of the "Good" Life 155
The Wider Dimensions of Heroism 159
The Power of "One(s)" 163
What Matters Most? 166
Reflecting on Retirement 170

Foreword
BY MICHAEL BRAUDE

Sheldon Stahl was a marvelous human being. He was a true liberal in every sense of that word. However, he had many very conservative folks who were friends and admirers.

One of my favorite memories of Sheldon is from a major civic banquet years ago in Kansas City, where Sheldon was seated among many dignitaries at the head table. As the Master of Ceremonies made introductions, he started to say "And to Sheldon's left…" then caught himself and added, "actually, there are very few to Sheldon's left." That was Sheldon.

I first got to know Sheldon when he was an economist at the Federal Reserve Bank of Kansas City. He was in demand as an articulate and well-informed speaker, and his keen sense of humor came through loud and clear. What set Sheldon apart was that he was truly a plain-talking economist. He literally made the dismal science interesting.

He was an accomplished scholar, serving as Dean of the School of Management at Rockhurst University in Kansas City, and as the Vernon Haase Professor of Business and Economics at Aurora University in Aurora, Ill. Dr. Stahl also had his own weekly radio show for more than five years on KCUR-FM, Kansas City's National Public Radio affiliate.

His work with UN-related organizations brought him into close contact with former U.S. Attorney General Eliot Richardson, and the two became fast friends. The bond between staunch Republican Richardson and strong Democrat Stahl was forged because both were kind, compassionate men. Their mutual respect as men of integrity was far grater than what divided them as members of two different parties.

A lot of us will miss Sheldon and his commentaries on domestic and global issues. These essays will remind us just how thoughtful he was.

What I personally miss most about Sheldon was his kind, sensitive, caring nature. He cared deeply about his family, his colleagues and his friends. He cared equally about the human race, particularly those who were victims of prejudice or poverty.

It was precisely those human qualities, which transcended political differences, that made Sheldon such an appealing person to all, regardless of political affiliation.

I am grateful that I will always be able to look up to Sheldon Stahl and consider him a wonderful friend and role model. Re-reading these essays is a marvelous way to rekindle his memory.

Michael Braude is the former president of the Kansas City Board of Trade.

Introduction

JOHN MARTELLARO, JAY SJERVEN, LOUANN STAHL

Sheldon W. Stahl was an uncommon economist. Far more meaningfully to the three of us, he was an uncommon human being.

He was an unapologetic liberal who spent much of his career working in the bastion of mainstream conservatism known as the Federal Reserve. His dear friend, the late Elliot Richardson, former U.S. Attorney General and author of *Reflections of a Radical Moderate,* used to tease Sheldon that he was the "moderate radical" to Richardson's "radical moderate."

He wore a suit and tie to work but had a laborer's appetite for effort—an inheritance no doubt from his father, a small business owner to whom Sheldon pays tribute in several of the essays that follow. Sheldon worked his entire life, although he "retired" not once, not twice, but from three different careers: as Vice President and Senior Economist at the Federal Reserve Bank of Kansas City; as the Vernon Haase Professor of Business and Economics at Aurora University in Aurora, Ill.; and finally as Resident Economist at Meara, King and Company, a Kansas City public accounting firm now known as Meara Welch Browne.

Sheldon was a gifted economist. Years before the credit collapse of 2008 and the resulting Great Recession, Sheldon saw it coming. As early as 2005, as one of the essays that follows shows, he was warning that the housing bubble and the arcane credit derivatives that fed off of it were unsustainable. Sooner or later, the piper would have to be paid. So many others said the boom could go on indefinitely; to their chagrin, Sheldon was proven right once again.

Sheldon was also a gifted, and giving, man. A teacher, a mentor, a leader, he was that rare and special individual who could get along with anyone, anytime, despite never compromising his principles.

It was during his years at Meara that he became an essayist, producing a series of columns for the firm's monthly client newsletter. A classic essayist, Sheldon poses a question or broaches a topic, then systematically, step by step, examines it from multiple sides as he works his way to a logical conclusion. He is the antithesis of the polemicists who now dominate the public debate.

Some of these essays, produced between 2004 and 2008, focused on the nuts and bolts of economic policy. Others were reflections on philosophy and life. We are grateful to the people at Meara for granting permission, and encouragement, for their republication in this volume.

In addition to numerous essays from his years at Meara, this volume also contains excerpts from speeches Sheldon delivered for and about some of the major institutions to which he devoted his time, talent and effort, including the United Nations Association of the U.S.A., and the Unitarian Universalist Church. It was Sheldon's tireless efforts on behalf of the United Nations, including service on several national UNA-USA committees and the international UNICEF board of directors, that established his relationship with Richardson, onetime president of the UNA-USA.

This volume offers the thoughtful reader a rich and rare worldview, the perspective of a man grounded in the gritty reality of the "dismal science" of economics, but leavened by a hopeful idealism that never wavered.

We considered it a rare honor to collect and review Sheldon's work and make the difficult choices required to produce a book-length volume. We offer it as a final tribute to an exceptional human being.

Prologue: Bridging the Divide
SEPTEMBER, 2007

Increasingly, our nation has been referred to as "divided." The last presidential election revealed to many a seemingly irreparable schism among the electorate. On one side were the "conservatives," reviled by many who did not subscribe to their political and/or social philosophy. On the other side were the "liberals," equally, if not more intensely reviled by those who saw them as unpatriotic and immoral. However, one must question whether this country is forever to be divided into two warring camps, talking past each other, with neither willing to pause and reflect on the possibility that there may be more that binds us together than separates us.

I believe that our country will never again be the United States of America if we allow ourselves to be manipulated by political operatives, whose clever use of language has deceived us into believing that our basic values and concerns are radically different from each other, rather than being more universally shared in nature. Would we not stop to help a neighbor in need, or a stranger, if they did not share our political preferences? Would we prohibit our children from playing together because of our differences? Is our sense of humanity with one another somehow conditioned upon what someone has told us makes us different? Or, can we see across that divide and recognize that, whatever our differences, we must share this fragile planet in common and work together to preserve it for ourselves and our posterity?

Neither political camp has a monopoly on goodness, or morality, or love of country. Our diversity has been used as a wedge to drive us apart, rather than allowing us to see that it is a source of our strength as a nation. "E Pluribus Unum," "From many, one," is more than a bit of Latin inscribed on our coinage. It is a reminder of the diverse people who came to these shores and subordinated their differences to forge a great nation. The great Emancipator, Abraham Lincoln, warned the nation as it was about to embark on a bloody civil war that "A house divided cannot stand." His admonishment should still resonate with us. If we are ever to bridge that which has been allowed to divide us, we must embrace inclusiveness and reject the entreaties of those who, for their own narrow and selfish gains, would seek to keep us divided. In Act III of Shakespeare's "The Merchant of Venice," the reviled character Shylock asks, "If you cut me, do I not bleed?" What was true of Shylock's plea for the recognition of his humanity is no less true of any of us. For, what may befall this divided nation will likely affect us all, and will not be undone if we remain divided. Or, may it not be the case that, in coming together and making manifest our shared values, we can leverage our strength and help to make our nation whole once again?

SECTION ONE:

BEHIND THE NUMBERS
Connecting Economics and Humanity

Behind the Numbers
FEBRUARY, 2009

There will always be a part, and always a very large part of every community, that have no care but for themselves, and whose care for themselves reaches little further than impatience of immediate pain, and eagerness for the nearest good.
—SAMUEL JOHNSON

Humanity is the keystone that holds nations and men together. When that collapses, the whole structure crumbles. This is as true of baseball teams as any other pursuit in life.
—CONNIE MACK

A human being is a part of the whole called by us universe, a part limited in time and space. He experiences himself, his thoughts and feelings as something separated from the rest, a kind of optical delusion of his consciousness. This delusion is kind of a prison for us, restricting us to our personal desires and to affection for a few persons nearest to us. Our task must be to free ourselves from this prison by widening our circle of compassion to embrace all living creatures and the whole of nature in its beauty.
—ALBERT EINSTEIN

Our current economic situation is grim indeed. The cost in terms of lost output and net wealth is already far beyond that which we have experienced in any previous post-World War II recession. And the rate of decline is accelerating, even as some legislators debate whether or not a sizable fiscal stimulus is necessary to "kick-start" economic growth. In the third quarter of 2008, the Gross Domestic Product (GDP) declined at an annual rate of 0.5 percent. However, the release of preliminary GDP data for the final quarter of 2008 showed that the economy had shrunk at the fastest pace in more than a quarter of a century—3.8 percent. Were it not for a substantial involuntary accumulation of inventories as a result of failing to cut production fast enough to keep pace with falling orders, the decline in GDP would have been at a rate of more than 5 percent. Although the economy slipped into a negative growth mode only in the last half of 2008, employment growth was negative throughout the year, with the final four months of 2008 accounting for 2 million lost jobs out of a total loss in jobs for the year of 2.6 million. And already in 2009, such major employers as Boeing, Microsoft, Intel, Sprint, Caterpillar, Macy's, Home Depot and others have announced layoffs totaling anywhere from 50,000-70,000 workers. A recent report from the Labor Department noted that while a record number of American workers–4.8 million—were drawing unemployment benefits as of mid-January 2009, this represented only 37 percent of those who were out of work.

But behind the mass of statistical data that serve to portray what well may be this worst of all economic/financial debacles since the Great Depression, there are countless human faces that bear tragic witness to its pain and adversity. As I pondered the enormity of the human costs already incurred, I was reminded of a television series that had aired more than half a century ago. The program was entitled *The Naked City* and was shot on location in New York City. It was a gritty police genre that focused on the effect of the crimes on ordinary people and the police officers investigating them. Rather than simply showing gratuitous violence, the series instead attempted to offer an insightful look into the lives of real human beings as their lives were affected by crime. I have never forgotten the tag line that was used at the close of each program, "There are eight million stories in the Naked City... this has been one of them." Similarly, our current economic travails reflect more than bloodless statistical data. Rather, they can offer opportunities for us to take a fuller measure of some of the tragic human costs that must be borne as a consequence thereof.

One such instance was brought to light by a recent TV news story that reported what happened to Marvin Schur, a 93-year old man from Bay City, Mich., retired and living on a fixed income. Schur was a World War II veteran, a widower, living alone in his modest home. Michigan, like much of the country from Texas eastward to the northeastern United States, had been in the grip of a ferocious winter storm that brought snow, sleet, and ice, along with deadly plunging temperatures. Schur fell behind in paying his electric bill, and the utility company limited his access to electric power by placing a device on his line that would automatically cut off power at a certain point. The device had a reset feature that could restore limited power, but it required the customer to go outside, exposed to the weather, in order to reset it. And, if the bill had not been paid by ten days after the "limiter" had been installed, all power would be cut off. Whatever might have been the circumstances that caused Mr. Schur to fall behind in his payment to the utility company, and/or his ability to understand that his power could be interrupted and what was required to restore it, the TV news story did not report. Neighbors grew concerned when they observed his windows had become covered with ice and, on investigation, his body was discovered. Alone, despite four layers of clothing and wrapped in a blanket, he had frozen to death in his home. Presumably, if he had the financial resources to pay his electric bill on time, he might still be alive. Nonetheless, it could be said that he was as much a victim of economic circumstances as he was of the bitter cold.

A second example is even more appalling in that there were numerous victims. The apparent motivation for this act was a sense of desperation that had its origins in a combination of a troubled mind and an overwhelming concern over economic survival. It drove an individual to commit a horrendous homicidal act. Far from the cold that had caused someone in economic distress to die of hypothermia, in the Wilmington area of Los Angeles, according to the Associated Press, "A father apparently distraught over job problems shot and killed his wife and five young children and then committed suicide at their home Tuesday, police said. The victims included two sets of twins." Ervin Lupoe, a 40-year old father, had been employed as a medical technician at a hospital. He recently had been fired from his job, was reported to have been deeply in debt and was, at the time of his act, a month behind on his mortgage payments. Would others in his same or similar circumstances resort to such a tragic act? Admittedly, Lupoe's act should be considered extreme. Nonetheless, desperate economic circumstances can and do trigger such responses, particularly when there is no one there to offer a helping hand or a caring and compassionate voice.

In the light of these two stories, we can speculate as to countless other such stories, each with their own human faces, that have gone unnoticed or unpublicized, and where an act of simple human kindness might have helped to give succor to someone at the edge of desperation. The economic underpinnings of such tragedies are painful, but we know that they are not without end. In time, our economy will surely heal. Still, it behooves us now to look within. Many if not most of us remain caught up in our frenetic lifestyles that assign such a high priority to "getting and spending." In embracing "consumerism," we may have struck a Faustian bargain. There is a real danger that we may have traded our humanity for the soulless acquisition of "things," becoming faceless and less caring to our neighbors and to our communities. It has been said that "humanity will one day be defined not by the gifts we possess but by the virtues we lack." Now, more than ever, our current crises offer us an opportunity to reach out and to regain that virtue of humanity that undergirds a civil society. That task is surely within our reach. For, as the internationally acclaimed spiritual teacher Marianne Williamson has observed, "In every community there is work to be done. In every nation, there are wounds to heal. In every heart there is the power to do it." Let the healing begin with us.

Rethinking Economics
MAY, 2008

Quite recently, I chanced to come across a document that first came to my attention more than twenty years ago. On November 13, 1986, the U.S. Conference of Catholic Bishops took final action in approving their pastoral letter entitled, *Economic Justice for All: Catholic Social Teaching and the U.S. Economy.* Throughout its gestation, the document was greeted with a mixture of approbation and criticism. The final draft of the pastoral letter was received with the same ambivalence. Its supporters would make the case that such a commentary was highly appropriate and a welcome addition to the discourse. Its detractors would argue that matters economic were outside the purview of the church, and that it might better stick to deliberations concerning the soul rather than with material concerns. Yet, this was certainly not the first time the church had made known its concerns over matters economic.

Historically, the progenitor to the pastoral letter was a papal encyclical written by Pope Leo XIII, published in 1891. Entitled *Rerum Novarum,* it spoke to the rights and duties of capital and labor. Coming as it did late in the industrial revolution then under way in our country, it acknowledged that "the spirit of revolutionary change (had) made its influence felt in the cognate sphere of practical economics." The encyclical made clear at the outset that "the discussion is not easy, nor is it void of danger. It is no easy matter to define the relative rights and mutual duties of the rich and of the poor, of capital and of labor." The papal concern over the plight of the working class and of the human dimensions and consequences of economic activities would be reflected nearly a hundred years later in the bishops' pastoral.

The pastoral appealed to one's faith "to measure this economy not only by what it produces, but also by how it touches human life and whether it protects or undermines the dignity of the human person." And, it went on to emphasize, "Economic decisions have human consequences and moral content: they help or hurt people, strengthen or weaken family life, advance or diminish the quality of justice in our land." In essence, the pastoral sought to put a human face on an economic system, the workings of which had profound implications for the quality of all those lives that were affected by decisions in the marketplace. In our current economic and social environment in which, oft times, working people are seen as cost centers whose welfare tends to be subordinated to maximizing short-term profitability, we have grown unaccustomed to giving ample consideration to the human consequences of the economic decisions made in an impersonal marketplace.

Thus, twenty years after the pastoral came to my attention, both as a professional economist and as a former academic dean at a local Jesuit university, I still find its content compelling and worthy of reflection. For, despite an economy that continues to grow, albeit more slowly than some months ago, low overall inflation, a low unemployment rate, and a stock market that by some measures is at an all-time high, there remains a prevailing sense of disappointment and discontent among many Americans who are of the opinion that the economy is not working very well for them and their families. To be sure, for many, there is a growing sense of outrage over meager real wage gains alongside high corporate earnings, continued upward trends in executive compensation, and job losses associated with outsourcing. For added insight as to the level of dissatisfaction over the economy, consider the words of Janet L. Yellen, President and C.E.O. of the Federal Reserve Bank of San Francisco, in a recent speech to the Center for the Study of Democracy at the University of California, Irvine:

> "…Over the past three decades, much of the gain from excellent macroeconomic performance has gone to just a small segment of the population—those already in the upper part of the distribution. As a result, inequality has grown. This inequality, coupled with increased turbulence in family incomes associated with job displacement and restructuring, sheds substantial light on the sources of disappointment and concern that show up in the opinion polls."

The point has often been made that "a rising tide lifts all boats." Thus, insofar as the economy is concerned, we have grown accustomed to measuring economic progress, or the lack thereof, by looking at such aggregate measures as the Gross Domestic Product (GDP) or the overall rate of unemployment. If the GDP rises or the unemployment rate declines, we may infer that we are doing well without reflecting at length, or at all, on just who this ubiquitous "we" really is. Yet at any given moment, there are, and always have been, both winners and losers as a consequence of what happens in the macro economy. What distinguishes the current scene is that despite more than five years of fairly good economic growth, there has been a growing sense, particularly among the middle class, that the economy does not seem to have been working to enhance their economic security or their economic wellbeing. And, as Ms. Yellen made clear in her address, there is ample statistical evidence to buttress such a view. In essence, reports on the GDP or the unemployment rate as well as other aggregate measures of economic performance may be seen as descriptive headlines largely devoid of human content. However, behind those headlines lies the rest of the story, and it is with that story that the bishops' pastoral concerns itself. For, it is that story that helps to focus our attention on the individual and societal consequences of the workings of our economic system.

It should be noted that the pastoral is both Catholic and catholic in nature. It is Catholic by virtue of its origin. It is, at the same time catholic because it concerns itself with issues that affect what is universal in human interest. This can be seen in the principal themes addressed in the letter. The first of these observes, "Every economic decision and institution must be judged in the light of whether it protects or undermines the dignity of the human person." A second theme states, "Human dignity can be realized and protected only in community." It reasons, therefore, that community, in turn, requires a broad social commitment to the *common* good. Thirdly, the pastoral asserts, "All people have a right to participate in the economic life of society." Thus, the demands of basic social justice require that people be given assurance of at least a minimum level of participation. A fourth theme asserts, "All members of society have a special obligation to the poor and vulnerable." But, rather than this giving way to pitting one group against another, the letter makes the case that the whole community might be strengthened by assisting those who are among the most vulnerable. The pastoral also makes note of the fact that Catholic teaching, as well as teachings of other religions, defines human rights as including not only civil and political rights, but economic rights as well that include food, clothing, shelter, rest, medical care, education, and employment, among others. And, it states that "human rights are the minimum conditions for life in community," and are, therefore, deserving of protection by society. Finally, the pastoral makes the point, "Society as a whole, acting through public and private institutions, has the moral responsibility to enhance human dignity and protect human rights."

In this day and age, when so many are so preoccupied with the "self," the bishops are deserving of our gratitude for reminding us that the sum of our economic system cannot be measured in dollars alone, a standard that all too often is employed by economists to the exclusion of other standards of value. Thus, it is appropriate to remind the reader that a not uncommon criticism of the discipline of economics has been that "economists often know the *price* of everything, but the *value* of nothing." By putting forward and lifting up the human and ethical dimensions of economic life, and by interjecting consideration of the inherent values that undergird conventional economics, the bishops have forced us into rethinking the way we look at economics, as well as our reciprocal responsibilities to one another in sustaining both the economy and human dignity.

On the Virtues of Being Transparent
NOVEMBER, 2004

I magine, if you will, a circumstance in which someone says to you, "I can see right through you." If you were like most people at the receiving end of such a comment, you would not likely take it as a compliment. Rather, it would be seen as an indication on the part of the messenger that he/she was of the opinion that your integrity and/or your motivation was subject to question, or of doubtful worth. However, as is quite often the case, words may be defined in a variety of ways, with the various meanings affording differing shadings or interpretations. In the case of the word "transparent," the meaning appears relatively unambiguous and without overtones that it should be construed as a pejorative or depreciatory in its meaning. The primary definition of the word is, "Having the property of transmitting rays of light, so that bodies can be seen through." Other alternatives reinforce that definition, such as, "readily understood; clear; easily detected; perfectly evident; guileless; and/or, free from pretense." Despite the fact that each of these definitions may be seen as virtuous when used to describe another being, for many people, being described as "transparent" conjures up a negative image. Yet even a casual examination of our business landscape, littered as it is with the wreckage of such former business icons as Enron and

Arthur Andersen, and with growing skepticism regarding the true financial and operating condition of a host of this country's most powerful enterprises, would suggest that what we have need of is greater transparency in the conduct and representation of these organizations to all their stakeholders.

When organizations lose their way and sink into an ethical morass, it typically does not reflect the failure of the chief executive alone. Rather, the tacit or explicit cooperation of others within the organization is also a necessary ingredient. Like a structure that is built on a shaky foundation and is destined to fall, an organization whose culture eschews transparency or promotes an environment that is marked by ethical shortfalls is also destined for a fall. For, just as form follows function, it is equally the case that organizational behavior follows culture. When we speak of the "culture" of an organization, we are referring to the values, traditions, attitudes, beliefs, and language that, taken together, guide and channel the behavior of those in the employ of the organization. While all businesses inevitably are at the mercy of the marketplace to assure their success, a flawed culture within an organization invariably is a good predictor of its demise; indeed, it may be a principal factor in the business' failure. Arguably, the actions of the chief executive officer and/or senior management clearly establish the cultural tone for an enterprise. It should, therefore, come as no great surprise that, when top management promotes a culture that favors opaqueness over greater transparency, and when its overriding goal is that of short-term profitability and stock price maximization over long-term health and profitability, trouble might not be far behind.

In today's complex and litigious business environment, we are far removed from a time when business between parties could literally be done on the basis of a "handshake." The growth in the scale and scope of modern business enterprises has resulted in added complexity to both the forms of those organizations and to our ability to fully comprehend the myriad accounting practices that we count on to accurately represent the true operating and financial condition of the business. In turn, this has promulgated an environment within which opportunists can more readily shield unethical practices from the full light of disclosure. In such a culture, where transparency and clarity are sacrificed for obtuseness and "creative" accounting practices, the public is surely the loser.

It may be instructive to recall that in medieval times, when knights in armor approached each other, as evidence of their good will, they would raise their visors with their right hand to reveal themselves and to indicate the absence of a weapon being drawn. This was an act of transparency, signifying good intentions and mutual respect and acknowledgment. It was, in fact, the precursor to the universal custom of the hand salute observed by military organizations around the world. Today, as we reflect upon the incivility and questionable business practices hidden from the cleansing light of day, we would do well to recall that medieval custom and the virtues of being transparent.

Let's Hear It for the Little Guy
MAY, 2007

On a number of occasions, while pondering the choice of a subject for my writing, I found myself literally "at a loss for words." Then, after a seemingly interminable period during which my "writer's block" appeared to have grown to an impenetrable barrier to any progress, I found myself confronted with several apparently disparate events that, when examined critically, come together to provide a focal point for exploration and elaboration. In this instance, in a single day I was privy to two occasions that triggered such an epiphany. The first of these occurred at a regular meeting of a breakfast club of which I am a member. Each weekly meeting features a guest speaker, and it has been our good fortune consistently to have articulate presentations about interesting subjects. At this particular meeting, the subject was the use of tax increment financing (TIF) as an incentive to attract private investment in community economic development efforts. It should be noted that the spate of downtown development in Kansas City was greatly aided and abetted by the use of TIFs, and was at the same time the source of considerable heated discussion regarding its virtues in the city's most recent mayoral race.

On the very same day of my breakfast meeting, my wife and I had the pleasure of attending an event that celebrated the 25th anniversary of a small, local, executive coaching/consulting firm. The founder of the firm is an old friend of more than thirty years. At the reception were many friends, colleagues, and highly satisfied clients from a number of local business firms, large and small. From their testimonials, it was clear that they had benefited from and were very appreciative of the services this firm provided. Reliable data attest to the fact that the road to survival for a new small business is strewn with obstacles. Only two-thirds of all new employer establishments survive at least two years, and that survival rate falls to 44 percent for firms that have managed to remain in business for at least four years. Yet, with a small complement of staff, including the firm's principals, my friend's firm had not only beaten the odds, but had thrived in arriving at the quarter century mark of longevity. Given the subject of my earlier breakfast meeting, it occurred to me that it had done so without the benefit of any TIF initiatives on its behalf. As I pondered that thought, I also reflected on the fact that this small firm was probably representative of countless similar small-to-medium-size firms in our community and elsewhere that contribute to our economic wellbeing without the dispensation of any incentives from their local government.

Whatever the merits or demerits regarding the use of TIFs, what is not subject to serious denial is that it is usually the case that such incentives typically are directed at larger rather than smaller economic players. And while the ostensible contributions of such players to the local economy tend to be highly publicized, the same cannot be said of the countless smaller firms that also contribute significantly to the wellbeing of their communities. In that regard, it is worth considering some of the impressive data coming from the Small Business Administration (SBA) that speak to the contributions of small-to-medium-size businesses to communities across our country. A June 2006 SBA release noted that small firms—those having fewer than 500 employees—employ about one-half of all private sector employees and pay more than 45 percent of the total private payroll in the United States. Perhaps most impressive is the fact that, over the past decade, of all the net new jobs created in the economy, small firms were responsible for from 60 to 80 percent of that number. Thus, despite the desire on the part of economic development bodies to tout the community benefits that would accrue if the incentives they employ are successful in landing the "big one," it surely might be worth reflecting upon what might ensue if more of their energies were expended on behalf of attracting and retaining small firms.

Writing some time ago on this subject, I made the point that, despite their sizable contributions to community wellbeing, many, if not most, of these smaller firms remain anonymous, except to their employees and to the neighborhoods and communities of which they are an integral part. Regrettably, we have become somewhat inured to the regular announcements of large-scale layoffs from among Fortune 500 companies. Thus, it is easy to overlook the fact that for this nation's smaller firms, while some layoffs have been inescapable, deep cuts in their work force have been resisted even in the face of weakened business conditions. Perhaps it is the costs associated with worker training that may weigh more heavily on the smaller firm than its larger, deep-pocketed corporate rivals that make it more sensitive to the virtues of job retention. Whatever the reasons, studies have demonstrated a greater sense of loyalty and obligation to their workforce and commitment to their communities by small-to-medium-size firms even though they must bear the added tax burden necessitated by various tax subsidies granted to the larger, more favored enterprises.

Any objective analysis of the economic development process undertaken by communities across this nation would reinforce the view noted earlier that incentives from local governments tend to flow much more readily to the larger economic players. To the extent that the far greater numbers of smaller players are largely taken for granted even in the face of the economic benefits they confer, perhaps the time is long overdue for us to more fully acknowledge that these businesses are well worth nurturing and keeping. As

I noted in an earlier writing on this subject:

> "It is not unusual that, at great cost, we tend to overlook those things of great value that are in plain sight, in order to hunt for what we perceive of as the greater prize. In these times of often harrowing change, to live in a community marked by stability and neighborliness is a great prize in and of itself. Shuttered plants and failed enterprises that formerly were homes to large numbers of workers dot this country's landscape, making hollow their promises of expanded growth and employment in return for incentives granted to them."

There is surely no denying the economic merits of those larger business entities whose presence and conduct have contributed greatly to our community. Often times, however, far more numerous smaller businesses have labored in their shadow, even as they, too, have helped to support the community with employment opportunities and with the taxes they pay. It seems only appropriate then, that we pause to recognize their ongoing efforts on our behalf. So, lest we forget, *"Let's hear it for the little guy!"*

On Making a Difference
JANUARY, 2007

There is, I suspect, deep within each of our souls an inherent hope that our time on this earth should be purposeful. That is, despite our sense of awareness that few of us will likely be the architects of significant transformative change, we do harbor at least the modest hope that our exertions might help to leave this earth a little better for future generations than we found it. At the same time, we also recognize that there have been many individuals who, over time, have been major positive change agents both during and subsequent to their lifetimes. Names such as Jesus, Galileo, DaVinci, Gandhi, Mother Theresa, King, Pasteur, Lister, Salk and many others are representative members of a vast pantheon of luminaries who have been recognized for their contributions to the enhancement of the human condition. How many more future contributors are laboring in obscurity we cannot know? However, from time to time, the honor roll expands as our society comes to recognize additional individuals whose efforts on behalf of humankind are seen as exemplary. One such person worthy of note is Muhammad Yunus, who was awarded the 2006 Nobel Peace Prize.

It has been said by the author Victor Hugo, "There is nothing so powerful as an idea whose time has come." History is replete with examples that attest to the truth of Hugo's observation. In our own country, for example, the institutionalization of discrimination in its various forms was forced to yield in the face of the civil rights movement. Similarly, the post-World War II decolonization of the former territories of European powers occurred as a consequence of the struggles for political independence, movements that championed the idea of freedom as an inherent right of all persons. Still, though we recognize the legitimacy of these ideas now, these ideas did not emerge full-blown, nor did they enjoy immediate success. Change by its very nature is disruptive. As a consequence, many ideas that have improved our lot have generated controversy and were vigorously resisted when they were first introduced. For, as Mahatma Gandhi observed, "First they ignore you, then they laugh at you, then they fight you, then you win." Thus, ideas are rather like a delicate seedling that is planted and must be nourished; it takes time before it flowers or grows to maturity. In the case of Muhammad Yunus, the idea that he championed seemed to many detractors at its outset to be counter-intuitive.

As a trained economist with a Ph.D. from Vanderbilt University, Yunus returned in the 1970s to his native Bangladesh, where, at the age of 34, he was appointed as head of the Department of Economics at Chittagong University. In 1974, a time when Bangladesh was experiencing severe famine, Yunus was inspired to take what was, at the time, a seemingly small personal action to help a few impoverished families. At the mercy of predatory lenders, the poor had little or no access to funds. In addition, interest rates were usurious, and the requirement that borrowers provide some form of collateral from their meager belongings essentially foreclosed the likelihood that a truly poor person could expect to borrow funds from such a source. What Yunus did was provide from his own funds a small personal loan in the aggregate amount of $27 to a group of 42 impoverished families that would allow them to produce a number of small items that they could sell in order to support themselves and their families. There was no requirement for collateral, and the borrowers were instructed simply to repay the loan when they could. From this humble initial gesture, there sprang the Grameen Bank or Bank of the Villages. Begun as a research project of his university to provide "microcredit," or loans in very small amounts, and other banking services to the very poor, the bank became enormously successful and a model for other financial institutions in other countries to utilize the avenue of microcredit to enable the poor to lift the yoke of poverty from their shoulders. According to recent online data, "The Bank continues to expand across the nation and still provides small loans to the rural poor. As of mid-2006, Grameen Bank branches number over 2,100. Its success has inspired similar projects around the world." Some other facts about the bank are noteworthy. For example, it is actually owned by its borrowers who hold some 94 percent of the total equity, with the government of Bangladesh holding the remaining 6 percent. Most of the borrowers—97 percent—are women, and the loan recovery rate is 98.85 percent.

From the humble initiative he undertook more than thirty years ago, Yunnus precipitated a revolutionary rethinking of the whole concept of developmental assistance. Rather than seeing the masses of poor people in one's country as a liability and a burden to be borne by society, the system of micro-lending begun by Yunus is premised on the idea that the nation's poor represent an underutilized asset with skills that can be made productive by providing them with access to small amounts of funding. In essence, in the place of a demeaning "hand-out" to the poor, micro-lending instead offers them a "hand-up" in the form of an entrepreneurial catalyst to help them become self-sufficient. In recognition of the extraordinary consequences that have flowed from what Yunus began in 1974, the United Nations designated 2005 as the International Year of Microcredit. And, in 2006, Muhammad Yunus and the Grameen Bank were jointly awarded the Nobel Peace Prize.

It is altogether fitting that, in seeking to reduce the degree of grinding poverty that so often is a causative factor in conflicts around the globe, adequate and long overdue recognition should be given to someone who truly has "made a profound difference" in the lives of so many. At the same time, let us take solace in the added recognition that even as we honor this one individual, there are countless others who continue to toil in anonymity to help in "making a difference" for generations yet to come.

Reaching Too Far?
APRIL, 2007

Ah, but a man's reach should exceed his grasp—or what's a heaven for?
—ROBERT BROWNING

Quite recently, an article in the *Wall Street Journal* caught my attention. It was entitled, "Starbucks Chairman Warns Trouble May Be Brewing as Chain Expands." The focus of the article was a concern on the part of its chairman, Howard Schultz, as to whether the "image" of this American corporate icon was in danger of being diluted as an unintended consequence of its ongoing pursuit of increased growth. In the article, Schultz makes the case that Starbucks' success and profitability rested upon creating a memorable "experience" for its customers that served to distinguish it from its rivals and allowed the firm to price its product at a significant premium vis-à-vis its competitors. That "experience" of which Mr. Schultz spoke was premised upon having dedicated people who personalized the Starbucks experience by knowing their customers' orders by heart, and by a relaxed and welcoming ambience that made customers comfortable in lingering over their coffee as long as they wished without feeling hurried. In a memo to executives, Schultz shared his concern that the drive for increased efficiency and growth had compromised the Starbucks experience. In turn, this posed the danger of reducing the Starbucks brand to little more than a commodity, and exposed it to being seen as no different from other coffee shops or fast food outlets.

It should certainly come as no surprise to readers that the pursuit of growth is very much an intrinsic component of the ethos of most, if not all, profit-seeking business firms. And, clearly Starbucks has been a highly successful and profitable business. Since it went public in 1992, it grew from 1,000 stores to 13,000 stores with a corporate vision that saw Starbucks as a global brand with 40,000 stores worldwide. Such aspirations as regards growth may be seen as the norm rather than the exception within the business community. Indeed, for many if not most firms, the idea that they must grow lest they die goes pretty much unchallenged, and within most conventional business literature, the advantages of growth have seldom been subject to serious rethinking. Thus, what is one to make of the Starbucks dilemma, the notion that growth may not be an unalloyed good and may well carry with it certain consequences that might compromise the prospects for long-term success or greater profitability?

The CEO Refresher bills itself as "a monthly newsletter on contemporary topics in creative leadership, competitive strategy, and performance improvement." John Abrams is the president of South Mountain Company, an employee-owned build/design firm with some thirty employees, located in Martha's Vineyard. Abrams is the author of a compelling piece entitled, "Challenging the Gospel of Growth," that recently appeared in the newsletter and that offered insights that may be helpful in thinking about benefits and/or costs associated with the pursuit of growth. Abrams shared some of his thoughts on the subject in the article:

"A cherished business doctrine is that growth must be a primary business purpose: 'Grow or perish' is a mostly unquestioned

> truth. At South Mountain we favor certain kinds of growth, but not expansion for its own sake. We embrace growth to achieve specific goals, but always with the consideration of the consequences: it may disrupt and endanger treasured qualities… We look for ways to develop and thrive without enlarging, thereby holding to limited growth…We think about 'enough' rather than 'more.'"

Indeed, it was that very consideration over the loss of "treasured qualities" in pursuing growth that motivated Howard Schultz of Starbucks to pen that memo in which he aired his concerns. Is growth pernicious? Is bigger always better? Can growth be reconciled without disrupting or endangering those defining "treasured qualities" that organizations seek to preserve?

It seems clear that there is no single, preordained scale that need apply uniformly to all business organizations. An arbitrary affinity to resist growth in size may make no more sense than a disposition to pursue unlimited expansion. Just as we are increasingly coming to question whether the environmental carrying capacity of the planet can accommodate unlimited growth, so, too, are we focusing on the distinction between "growth" and "development." Abrams refers to the respected economist Herman Daly, who makes clear that our concern over the adverse consequences of excessive growth need not mean that a firm must limit its development. He notes that growth implies an actual increase in size or scale, while to develop means "…to expand or realize the potentialities of: to bring to a fuller, greater or better state…" In essence, we can work continually to get better without necessarily getting bigger. And, to further clarify that distinction, Daly observes that, "Our planet develops over time without growing, while our economy, a subsystem of the finite and nongrowing earth, must eventually adapt to a similar pattern."

Thus, in returning to a consideration of the Starbucks dilemma noted earlier, it should be clear that the real issue should not be framed in terms of "growth" versus "no growth." Rather, it is far more helpful to focus our attention on the "quality" dimensions of growth as opposed to its pace or magnitude. In this regard, John Abrams offers us valuable touchstones to guide us in our deliberations. He writes:

> "Some things we want to grow and some we do not. We want to increase our responsiveness, our satisfaction, our effectiveness, our reputation, our legacy, our sense of accomplishment, our relevance, our capacity to improve the quality of our products, and our contributions to good lives for our employees and our community. We do not want to increase our waste, our pollution, our unfulfilled commitments, our stress levels, or our callbacks."

Regrettably, for many publicly owned business organizations, the relentless impetus to push for more growth in order to maximize short-term earnings and placate shareholders has led to a Faustian bargain that has made them bigger, but not necessarily better. At the same time, an unwillingness on the part of many firms to "make the numbers," irrespective of the longer-term consequences, has led them to return to private ownership where they are less constrained in seeking to become "better," not simply "bigger," and where concern for the bottom line might as likely include a consideration of "enough" as opposed to an exclusive preoccupation with "more." The April 2, 2007 issue of Fortune magazine highlights just such a firm, Patagonia, a highly successful and environmentally aware outdoor clothing and equipment company. However, whether a company is publicly owned or private, a good rule to observe in seeking an appropriate balance in the quest for profitability is to avoid "reaching too far," only to find that the prize may not be worth what must be paid in attaining it.

The United Nations at 60: A Balance Sheet
MAYOR'S UNITED NATIONS DAY DINNER
OCTOBER, 2005

In the preamble to the United Nations Charter, one of the purposes of the U.N. was cited as, "…to save succeeding generations from the scourge of war." By that standard, one might be of the opinion that, after nearly sixty years since its inception, the United Nations has proved to be a failure. After all, while a conflagration similar to World Wars I or II has been avoided, a host of more localized wars plagued humankind during that same period. Yet, it would be wholly unfair to conclude that the U.N. has failed the world. Rather, it might be more appropriate to ask whether the world had failed the U.N. For in the final analysis, the U.N. is only capable of exercising that power that has been granted it by the member states. And regrettably, nation states have been reluctant either to give up what they perceive are elements of their sovereignty or provide the resources adequate to permit the U.N. to more fully discharge its responsibilities.

Nonetheless, an accounting of the record of the United Nations over the decades would show far more plusses on the balance sheet than minuses. To be sure, the minuses, though fewer in number, always seem to loom larger in the eyes of the U.N.'s critics than do its accomplishments. Still, one must acknowledge that those apparent failings that have gained notoriety recently have hurt the reputation of the U.N. and provided fodder to its critics. The report of the body headed by Paul Volcker made clear that the Iraqi Oil-for-Food program was badly managed and tainted by corruption. This was a U.N. failing. But it should be noted that the program itself was designed by the United States and Great Britain. They wrote the rules that made it possible for Saddam Hussein to capitalize on programmatic shortfalls, and it was they who failed to stop the smuggling activities that were a major source of Iraq's illegal revenues. Surely both the U.S. and the U.K. should share responsibility along with the U.N. official who headed the program. Similarly, the failure of the U.N. to stop the killing in Rwanda must be acknowledged. At the same time, it was at the behest of the U.S., U.K. and France, that the U.N. peacekeeping mission there remained neutral, a constraint that effectively inhibited the degree to which peacekeepers could project any force to stop the killing. Nonetheless, allegations of sexual exploitation and abuse of minors by U.N. peacekeepers in the Congo tarnish the reputation of the U.N., as do allegations of sexual harassment by the head of the U.N. High Commission for Refugees.

Such failings must not be seen in a vacuum, however. They occur because, like all institutions, the U.N. is imperfect; it remains a work in progress. And the actions of individuals who are fallible should not necessarily be taken as a sign that the entire U.N. is at fault. Indeed, a partial list of the U.N.'s accomplishments would far outweigh its failings. For example, since 1948, U.N. peacekeepers have been called upon some 59 times and currently maintain 16 peacekeeping operations, a testament to their value as seen by those who have called for them. During that time, the "blue helmets" were awarded a Nobel Peace Prize for their efforts. The ongoing work of UNICEF on behalf of the world's children and their parents has also earned that body a Nobel Prize, as has the High Commission for

Refugees. The World Health Organization (WHO) has limited the scourge of smallpox, while the Food and Agricultural Organization (FAO) has helped improve agricultural methods, enhanced global food safety, and distributed food around the world as needed. And on and on the list of accomplishments could go.

In assessing the U.N.'s record over nearly 60 years, we must remember that it is not a world government that can issue mandates to the world's citizens. Rather, it is made up of 191 sovereign nations, and has only the resources that the member states choose to give to it. In reality, that collective body of nation states has been far more aggressive in tasking the U.N. with responsibilities than it has with providing it with the needed resources to fully and effectively discharge those responsibilities. Still, whatever might be its shortcomings, it has been said on more than one occasion that if the U.N. did not exist, it would have to be invented. In a world growing ever more interdependent, neither the world's problems nor their solutions can be expected to be limited to any single nation or small group of nations. Global cooperation is needed to deal with global problems, and the U.N. is the only truly global entity at the world's disposal. To acknowledge its failings is something that we should not be loath to do. Rather, to recognize its imperfections and to resolve to reform the institution for the better is what is needed. In that spirit, we should welcome the report of the High Level Panel on Threats, Challenges and Change, issued on December 2, 2004, in response to the call by Secretary-General Kofi Annan to examine the ways in which the U.N. might be reformed to better deal with the crucial issues facing the global community.

Finally, I believe that in the heart of humankind lies the key to a "transformative paradigm" that ultimately must acknowledge the biblical admonition that we are indeed, our brothers' keepers. It is incumbent upon us to work hard in support of the United Nations to make it the prime vehicle to make manifest that transformation.

On Globalization: The Rest of the Story
MARCH, 2006

One of America's radio icons over the years has been Paul Harvey. He is a raconteur—a storyteller—who is very skilled in what he does, and his stories are typically told in two parts. In the first part, he engages the listeners' attention and interest as he builds towards his closing observations that, more often than not, contain a surprising or unexpected twist. Before the audience is privy to his closing remarks, there is a timely commercial pause, and when Paul Harvey returns to finish his story, he prefaces his remarks to come with the tag line, "And now, the rest of the story."

Of globalization, we have heard much in recent years. And, one might be excused for having concluded that in the globalization story, despite the recognition that for many American workers it has meant pain and displacement, the winners far outnumber the losers. In terms of sheer numbers, that is undoubtedly true. Most assuredly, the growing economic inter-connectedness and rapid growth of trade between nations has brought with it for legions of America's consumers tangible benefits in the form of a wider array of high-quality goods and services at lower prices than might otherwise have prevailed. And foreign direct investment in the United States has provided employment for millions of workers. For example, "insourcing" in such U.S. industries as automobile manufacturing has created tens of thousands of relatively high-paying jobs for American workers, helping to offset the downsizing and layoffs experienced by old line domestic auto producers. In so doing, that foreign investment has brought vitality and renewed hope to whole regions of our country that have been witness to a wholesale contraction and the outsourcing or "offshoring" of their manufacturing base.

Likewise, we should recognize and applaud the fact that in countries like China and India, as well as in other developing countries, globalization has raised up many millions of people out of dire economic circumstances. They have been given both the hope and the means to enjoy a better life for themselves and their children, enabling large numbers of them to become members of a growing middle class of citizens. Although it remains true that our huge and growing trade deficit is a testament to the seemingly inexhaustible demand for imported goods on our part, that growth in U.S. imports has provided foreigners with the wherewithal to fuel a substantial and growing appetite for U.S. exports as well. Thus, for the world as a whole, as well as in our own country, ought not we conclude that the globalization story ends with the tag line, "And, they all (or most) lived happily ever after?" Or, if one looks at the subject more expansively, might there be more to "the rest of the story?"

Quite recently, noted author and champion of globalization Thomas Friedman published his second book on the subject. His first book, *The Lexus and the Olive Tree,* documented the rise of information technology that was knitting the world more closely together, led by companies whose reach for new markets and for labor was growing more global in its scope. In his latest book, *The World is Flat: A Brief History of the Twenty-First Century,* Friedman makes the case that the massive investment boom in

IT and bandwidth capacity during the decade of the 1990s provided the means to knit the world even more closely together. As a consequence, the pace of globalization greatly accelerated, and in its wake was a worldwide economic and financial playing field that had been flattened and that, in Friedman's words, "allows for multiple forms of collaboration without regard to geography or distance—or soon, even language." To the extent that this is an accurate characterization of the global economic landscape, globalization may be likened to an all-encompassing wave sweeping the earth. And, to a non-critical observer, as that wave continues its sweep generating ever-growing levels of trade and economic activity, it may, indeed, "lift all boats." However, before subscribing to that conclusion, there are questions that need to be considered. Among them, are the consequences of such growth wholly beneficial? And, can the pace of global economic activity continue to be sustained?

Globalization has presented us with an ever-changing and increasingly intense competitive environment. To the extent that all change by nature is disruptive, this may seem like disruption "on steroids." Within our own country, we have already noted the shrinking manufacturing base as more and more work has been outsourced overseas in the non-ending search for lower costs of production. Added to the ranks of our unemployed manufacturing workers are growing numbers of workers in formerly well-paid technical and professional areas whose jobs also are migrating overseas. Thus, in addition to a growing sense of frustration over the loss of jobs here, there has been a corresponding increase in a feeling of insecurity and foreboding over what the future may hold for the displaced workers and their families. There is a growing fear, buttressed by more than anecdotal evidence, that the gains for workers in developing countries are coming at the expense of, rather than in concert with, workers gains in advanced industrial countries. And this scenario is taking root in other advanced industrial countries as well, igniting more than just a hint of xenophobia both here and abroad.

In addition to questions over the size and the distribution of the gains from trade, there are also more fundamental concerns over the very sustainability of the ongoing increase in global economic activity. Whether one subscribes to the "peak oil" hypothesis or not, the dramatic increase in demand occasioned by globalization presupposes a commensurate increase in the capacity to accommodate that demand as well as a huge increase in overall economic activity. Yet, a vital element of that capacity increase is the availability of reliable energy resources at prices/costs that do not serve as an impediment to such growth. One does not have to be an expert in the field to understand that the era of cheap and abundant energy resources is gone, and that the future outlook will be one of growing scarcity and higher prices. Although technological advances may help to ameliorate this problem, we also have learned that technological change is not without unintended and frequently adverse consequences of its own. At the same time, as more and more people throughout the world seek to emulate the conspicuous consumption and the excessive materialism that are characteristic of our country and other developed nations, the increased economic activity to accommodate those aspirations will almost certainly entail added environmental pollution. This will mean an increase in the emissions of those greenhouse gasses that have been responsible for the "global warming" phenomenon that is already seriously affecting our planet. Is the collective will to tackle this problem commensurate with the magnitude of the challenge it poses for us and our posterity? Will our faith and hope in the efficacy of technology to come to our rescue be rewarded in a timely manner before an environmental "tipping point" is reached?

I do not pretend to know the answer to these and/or other related questions, but they should be asked nonetheless. However, to ask them is not to disparage the prospects for positive change and global economic growth and progress. And there are many more questions that could well be raised. Rather, this exercise is meant to raise our sensitivity to the fact that the changes that are under way and that may yet await us carry with them both risks and rewards. If change itself is inevitable, the content of that change is not immutable, for we are the change agents. What we choose to do as regards our future will profoundly affect that change for good or ill. In a world that surely will be marked by an intensification of economic *competition,* paradoxically, it may well be that the hopes for a richer and more secure future may depend upon an ethic of mutual *cooperation* to solve the problems posed by globalization. Globalization has presented us with a need to critically address a host of questions the answers to which have yet to be resolved. In that sense, it might seem somewhat presumptuous to offer as a sub-title to a book, "A Brief History of the Twenty-First Century," well before the first decade of that century has passed. Extrapolation based on such a short span of events seems hardly a reliable guide to an uncertain future. The story of the twenty-first century is yet to be written. Whether the globalization wave proves to be the precursor to that "tide that lifts all boats," or whether its costs to society far exceed its benefits remains to be seen. We should all stay tuned "for the rest of the story."

Through the Efforts of Others
FEBRUARY, 2007

A short time ago, I received an e-mail from a good friend that piqued my interest. The "subject" box read, "a note about parachutes" and related to a story that concerned Charles Plumb, a naval aviator during the Vietnam War, who had to bail out from his aircraft that had been hit by a surface-to-air missile. He was captured and endured some six years of harsh imprisonment. Following his release at the end of the hostilities, he returned home and took to the lecture circuit as a motivational speaker, drawing upon the lessons he had learned from that horrific experience. The e-mail went on to chronicle a chance meeting that Plumb had while sitting in a restaurant with his wife. A man approached Plumb and recounted to him that he recognized him as a jet fighter pilot who had flown from the carrier Kitty Hawk during the Vietnam War and who had been shot down. When Plumb inquired as to how he could possibly know those facts, the gentleman informed him that as a crew member on that carrier, he had actually packed Plumb's parachute, the very same chute that saved Plumb's life when he ejected from his crippled plane. From this extraordinary encounter, in which Plumb was face-to-face with the person who had literally held his life in his hands, he recognized and reaffirmed a simple truth: Whatever he accomplished in life was not as a result of his exertions alone. Rather, it was dependent upon the work of others along the way as well. And, in his public presentations, he makes a point of asking his audiences, "Who's packing your parachute?" as a reminder of the debt we owe to countless others for their contributions to our own successes.

I suspect that many of us do not regularly indulge in the act of self-assessment. However, if we did, it would not be surprising to find that our opinion of ourselves, more often than not, would likely be complimentary. That is to say, if we stopped to take a critical look at ourselves and what we have accomplished in our lifetimes as adults, we might well give ourselves a pat on the back for whatever success we have enjoyed. And, in meting out this self-praise, many undoubtedly would credit the attribute of self-reliance as playing a major, if not the major, role in their accomplishments. For, the myths about pulling oneself up by the bootstraps and the "self-made" man enjoy a particular resonance in our business-oriented culture. Yet, all of us surely must, at the same time, recognize and acknowledge that, throughout our lives, we have profited from having been the beneficiaries of the efforts and/or the kindnesses of others.

We readily accept that verity when it comes to how we observe certain team sporting events. No matter the inherent brilliance or talents of any single player, neither that player nor that team could readily succeed were it not for the cooperation and collaboration of all of the team members. On occasion, I am sure that we may have been witness to an event where a "star" may seemingly take the outcome of the game into his or her hands and deliver one of those rare performances where, through what seems like an individual act of sheer will, one player shapes the outcome of the contest. I can recall having had such an experience in witnessing Michael Jordan of the Chicago Bulls basketball team do just that in a 1998 NBA championship game against the Utah Jazz. Nonetheless, even as we might acknowledge the exceptional talent of an individual, we also must realize that the final outcome was a function of the contributions of other team members as well. Likewise, though our market-based economy may laud the virtues of competition among firms in determining the ranks of winners and losers in the relentless hunt for profitability, more astute business executives have come to recognize the virtues of the "team" and the synergies that derive from the collaborative/cooperative efforts of the team members who collectively make up the organization. If they should choose to ignore that truth, they do so at their peril. A couple of examples may serve to drive home that lesson.

Louis Uchitelle is an economics reporter for *The New York Times* and the author of a recent book entitled, *The Disposable American: Layoffs and Their Consequences*. Michelle Conlin reviewed the book for Business Week magazine and noted: "…Uchitelle's book is about what he views as the folly of the modern layoff—one of the inevitable results of an economy designed for nonstop expansion. …This culture, in which employees are treated as if they had sell-by dates, has huge, oft ignored costs…"

Conlin observed that Uchitelle cited evidence to make the case that CEOs of more enlightened firms such as Southwest Airlines and Harley-Davidson, which eschew the layoff palliative, reap the rewards of higher profitability from a fiercely loyal workforce that generates higher productivity and superior innovation. And in an economy in which stock performance is regarded by many as the sine qua non or touchstone of an executive's prowess, Conlin writes, "…Uchitelle draws upon mounds of research to show that slashing staff in the name of growth does not, in the long run, lead to better stock performance." If the workforce in its entirety is the "team" that contributes positively to a firm's long-term profitability and to the reputation of the CEO, it follows that one should proceed with extreme caution before discounting the contributions of the employees or wielding the layoff weapon.

Writing in the January 15, 2007, issue of *Business Week,* Brian Grow recounted the events leading up to the resignation of Robert Nardelli, formerly the CEO of Home Depot. Notwithstanding some erosion of the financials at Home Depot associated with the slowdown in the housing sector, Nardelli's "numbers were quite good," according to analyst Matthew J. Fasler of the Goldman Sachs Group. Still, the article noted that Nardelli's management style was the source of "…a quivering anger that his arrogance provoked within every one of his key constituencies; employees, customers, and shareholders…." Indeed, the article noted, as a consequence of staffing cuts he made to restrain costs, "…Nardelli alienated customers as thoroughly as he did employees." For a company with a large "do-it-yourself" customer base that required hands-on assistance from the staff, this was a serious error in judgment that, in 2005, precipitated Home Depot's fall to last place among major U.S. retailers in a prestigious survey of consumer satisfaction conducted annually by the University of Michigan. And as one irate shareholder said, "You can't s—t on your employees and deliver results."

Whatever might be the technical or financial acumen of business executives, there is a lesson that surely is applicable to a far wider audience. It has been said that, "success has many fathers, but failure is an orphan." Whether through inadvertence or arrogance, when we presume to think that our successes are a product wholly of our own doing, ignoring or discounting the contributions of countless others, we may find ourselves vulnerable to being knocked off the lofty perch we believe we should occupy. For as we go about our daily business, our lives are continually touched by and affected by the actions and kindnesses of others, many of whom remain anonymous to us. Our characters are forged from many disparate ingredients, but surely among the most important of them is humility. And so, as we celebrate our triumphs, we would do well always to remember to extend assistance and kindness to others we may encounter, as a sign of our humility and in recognition that our own journey has been made easier for us in no small measure "by the efforts of others."

Who Wants to be a Millionare?
MAY, 2006

Most readers are familiar with the wildly popular television quiz show that bears the same name as this article. For a very fortunate few, millionaire status may be only sixteen questions away from realization. For others, in recent years, thanks to stock options and a surging stock market, or to entrepreneurial success in the high-flying world of the internet-based "dot coms," their dream of becoming millionaires has been realized with growing success. But, what of those countless numbers of people for whom the dream remains elusive? What advice might we tender that could be helpful in moving them towards the wealth to which they may aspire?

It should be noted that in recent years more and more Americans have achieved a net worth in excess of one million dollars. It should also be noted that, at the same time, the gap between those who have much and those who live in poverty has grown ever wider. As a success-oriented society, it is not surprising that more attention is directed to the former group than to the latter. In that regard, a recent book by Thomas J. Stanley and William D. Danko entitled "The Millionaire Next Door: The Surprising Secrets of America's Wealthy" has enjoyed great success. Based upon twenty years of interviewing those who had attained millionaire status, Stanley and

Danko postulated a number of common denominators that appear to be present among those in that growing financial fraternity. These included living well below their means; managing their time, energy and money in ways conducive towards building wealth; shunning displays of high social status; a proficiency in targeting marketing opportunities, and choosing the right occupation. In point of fact, in asking the question, "Who becomes wealthy?" the authors state, "Usually the wealthy individual is a businessman who has lived in the same town for all his adult life." I believe that the key here is that most self-made millionaires are in business for themselves, rather than someone's employees.

If this seems to be the case, is there any practical advice that might be offered to struggling entrepreneurs that could help them to stay on the straight and narrow path to achieving financial independence? Here are several suggestions for avoiding failure and for achieving success in one's own business. In each case, it is helpful to remember the three (3) *P's*. To minimize the prospects for business failure, it is important that you avoid striving for *Perfection*. *Perfection* is seldom, if ever, attainable, and the energy spent in its pursuit invariably leads to *Procrastination,* delaying decision-making, and/or *Paralysis,* a failure to choose more productive and rewarding paths to business success. At the same time, those factors helping to maximize the prospects for business success include *Positioning, Performance, and Persistence. Positioning* involves not only knowing your customers' needs, but also making sure that your offering(s) uniquely satisfy those needs and create value for the customer. *Performance* refers to keeping your promises and standing behind any representations you have made to your customers. *Persistence* speaks for itself. It involves doggedly persevering in trying to distinguish yourself from among the pack, and seeking new and better ways to constantly improve the offerings of your business.

To be sure, in business as in life, there are no ironclad guarantees of success. Certainly, knowing and avoiding those things that are conducive to failure is a good starting point. At the same time, practicing those traits that are associated with a higher likelihood of success also would seem to be an inherently wise choice. Thus, if and when you may be asked, "Who wants to be a millionaire?" if that should be your choice, make sure that your final answer reflects an awareness of just what it takes to get there and a willingness to stay the course in pursuit of that prize. Unlike TV quiz shows, for most of us, anything to which we truly aspire requires that it must be earned through hard work; it is seldom, if ever handed to us.

Putting Your People First: It Makes Dollars and Sense
MAY, 2006

Of all the problems with which businessmen and women have to contend, perhaps one of the most vexing has been the increasing difficulty in finding *and* keeping people with the requisite skills in the face of tightening labor markets. Although employers have demonstrated considerable ingenuity in coping with this problem, nonetheless, it remains a very challenging task for them to manage. In the face of such difficulties, the value of having productive *and* dedicated employees would seem to be quite obvious. But, with such employees at a premium and coveted by competitors, what can one do to tilt the odds in your favor when it comes to retaining those workers? The answer to this question may be as simple as, "putting your people first."

Whether your employees are on the front line in serving your customers or behind the scenes in the production process, it should be apparent that the attitude they bring with them to the workplace each day is a key ingredient in the success and profitability of your business. While it remains true that the ultimate *end* of any profitable business is to serve its customers, it is equally true that the employees are the *means* to serve that end. Does it not, therefore, make sense that, by creating a workplace environment that inspires loyalty and dedication on the part of those employees, you will raise their commitment level to do whatever is necessary to make customers happy? The ultimate success of your business depends upon serving your customers better than your competitors. And, your employees should be seen as key players in that process. If your business is seen by your employees as a place that *cares about them,* and is willing to invest in those things that will make them more content and productive, you should expect that they will more readily *care about you* and will strive better to serve your business and its customers. This is nothing more than recognizing that the manner in which you treat those who work for you will go a long way in determining *how* they work for you.

The reality of today's and tomorrow's workplace is that the skills and competencies of workers will have to be continually upgraded if a business expects to be successful over the long run. Business managers have long understood that investing in training and technology is indispensable for maintaining a competitive edge. Thus, such an investment in people to better equip them to do their jobs, though costly, is in the employer's self interest. What should be equally apparent is that accommodating your employees' needs for such things as transportation, day care, flexible work schedules, and for a caring and concerned workplace environment, is also self-serving for the business owner. Today's tight labor markets have forced many employers grudgingly to accept such obligations as unavoidable costs. However, astute employers should realize that, within reason, whatever they can do to show their appreciation for the efforts of their workers will reap them significant and enduring benefits. Putting their people first *is* good business.

Some Reflections on Avarice and Generosity
SEPTEMBER, 2006

Some time ago, I wrote an essay entitled, "How Much Is Enough?" In the introductory paragraph, I provided an example in which my wife and I admonished one of our then very young daughters not to take "too much" when she was offered a tempting treat of some sort. It should come as no surprise, given she was a very young child, her reaction was contrary to that which we sought. Thus for her, "too much" became the forbidden fruit and the measure of her desire. And, when she was offered something that appealed to her, and was asked how much she would like to have, her answer would invariably be, "Too much." I make mention of that essay because of several recent events, one of which caused me to ponder the consequences of conduct that eschews reasonable bounds and that elevates excess to a level of acceptability that is both unwise for us as individuals and injurious to us as a society. On the other hand, I had the privilege of meeting an individual whose character and conduct was such that it made my spirit soar with a renewed sense of optimism.

One might well ask what the above example of a child's inability to resist temptation has to do with avarice, one of the so-called "seven deadly sins." In consulting my well-worn Webster's New Collegiate Dictionary, I found the word "avarice" defined as an *"inordinate desire for wealth; implying both miserliness and greed."* In turn, "greed" is defined as *"...acquisitive desire beyond reason."* Surely, we would be loath to describe a small child's excessive desire for something as reflective of avarice or greed. For the very young lack a well-developed and mature faculty of reasoning, a prerequisite for making informed judgments as to what is or is not beyond reason. Although both children and adults may make poor choices, the burden of responsibility for making such choices falls more heavily upon the shoulders of adults, for they have both the experience and the faculty to subject choices to the test of reasonableness.

To be sure, discerning that which is reasonable from that which is not introduces an element of subjectivity into the matter. For what may strike one as eminently reasonable may be seen by another as beyond the pale. And yet, each one of us regularly grapples with making such judgments, despite the absence of an incontrovertible standard that, under all circumstances, would define what constitutes reasonable behavior. What one can say with a high degree of assurance is that when avarice is being practiced, it is the welfare of the individual or of some individuals that is being advanced rather than the welfare of the broader community. A recent meeting I attended featured a speaker on the subject of executive compensation. His remarks offered a strong indictment of the greedy mindset that seems to be all too common in both the public and private sectors within our country. The speaker provided an insightful presentation on the growing disparity between compensation received by average workers and the compensation of senior corporate executives. Among the advanced industrial countries of the world, the disparity was widest in the United States. Repeatedly, executives in their zeal to reward themselves to the fullest sacrificed the interests of their workers and shareholders so that they themselves might prosper, often compromising the very viability of their company itself in the process. This message was delivered to a room full of businessmen who were sensitive to the injustice that was being perpetrated in order to excessively enrich the few at the expense of the many. Although those in attendance might not necessarily agree on a single measure of what constituted avarice, "they could recognize it when they saw it." And when the speaker suggested that market capitalism itself might fail if the cult of avariciousness was not brought under control, there were few, if any, members of the audience who voiced any disagreement.

That the sway of avarice is strong, and that its consequences ultimately tend to be hurtful to those who practice it and to the broader community, should come as no surprise. In addition to the examples cited by the breakfast speaker, we have seen it at work in our society when executives from the major tobacco companies testified in lock step before Congress that their industry was not being deceptive in denying the addictive nature of their product or of the harm it causes. Similarly, when in the name of profit maximization, major pharmaceutical companies compromise the health and safety of their customers by failing adequately to inform the users of their products of potentially life-threatening side effects, avarice is at work. And confronted with hard scientific evidence of the detrimental effects of human activities on the very health of the planet that sustains us, when those responsible fail to curb such activities, we are witnessing avarice and irresponsibility on a mega-scale. Surely, readers could readily add many other examples of their own choosing.

We live in a culture that has elevated acquisitiveness to a way of life, and having the wherewithal to indulge that habit provides the temptation to focus on "getting and spending." And in the "getting" part of that equation, individuals and organizations may often step over the line that separates desire from avarice. At the same time, lest we conclude that our society may be irredeemably marching down a path that continues to elevate the "self" over the "selfless," let me share some insights into the character of someone

I was recently privileged to meet, whose generosity and philosophy of life is truly inspirational and uplifting and may serve as an antidote for the virus of avarice.

It has been said that the human capacity for self-delusion is nearly limitless. This is surely true when it comes to one's profession of faith and spirituality. Lots of people "talk the talk" but fail to "walk the walk." When you meet someone who represents "the real goods," it is a humbling experience. The gentleman I met is an octogenarian who seems to have boundless energy and an infectious smile and disposition. His small precision tooling company employs perhaps a dozen people, but at a time when the term "job security" more and more seems like an oxymoron, he takes great pride in the fact that a number of his employees have been with the firm for four decades with others having a decade or more with the company. He was quick to confess that he considered himself blessed to have experienced business success, readily crediting that success to employees that take pride in doing a job right, as well as to his deeply rooted faith that has had a lasting effect on his actions and his life. When asked about his business philosophy, he noted that, "Our motto is Good Work at a Fair Price on Time," which he explained was prompted by the biblical verse in Ephesians 6:7 that reads, "With good will doing service, as to the *Lord,* and not to men."

As his business has grown and prospered since it was founded in 1959, his faith has been manifest in his work with troubled youth and prison ministries, among many other worthy causes. That same faith and generosity of spirit also is reflected in charitable giving far above and beyond what would normally be considered as tithing. In that regard, he commented that he never gave in order to get something in return. Rather, his giving was in response to his own good fortune as he observed that, "I can't give that which was not given to me." And, he confessed that, despite that which he gives, he is not altogether surprised to find himself with more at the end of a year than at its beginning, directing me to Proverbs 11: 24-25, which affirms the ageless notion of "doing well by doing good."

Largely-self-taught and with no academic degrees, with a life partner he met in Bible school who has been his wife for 61 years, and with enormous pride in his four grown children and nine grandchildren, this is a man whose life of faith and generosity stands in stark contrast to the previous examples of avarice. In a world with far too much cynicism and greed, it is very hard to withhold admiration for this principled man whose humility and generosity may serve as a model for the rest of us, encouraging us simply "…to aspire to do the right thing for its own sake." For in doing so, we may rediscover what this extraordinary gentleman has long known, namely, that in giving of ourselves unselfishly, we are rewarded many times over.

The Long and the Short of It
OCTOBER, 2006

The renowned British economist John Maynard Keynes made the observation that, "The long run is a misleading guide to current affairs. In the long run, we are all dead." Yet, Keynes was very much concerned with the long run. However, in challenging the economic orthodoxy of the day at a time of global economic depression, Keynes argued that the depressed state of the economy was due to an inadequacy of demand in the private sector that could be remedied by having the public sector, or government, increase demand in the marketplace by running a deficit, rather than waiting for private market forces to do the job in some more distant period. Unfortunately, it is likely that people are more apt to recall his admonition without recalling the context in which he made it.

Regrettably, it appears as though our willingness to favor the short run over longer-run considerations may well be the root cause of many of our most pressing problems. Consider the conduct of publicly traded business corporations to maximize short-term profits. This had led to numerous instances of aggressive and illegal accounting practices that have compromised the long-run viability of those corporations. Similarly, as consumers we seek instant gratification in getting things *now,* not by means of saving for such purchases, but rather through piling on ever larger amounts of debt, hopefully to be repaid at some time in the future. In the public arena, politicians irrespective of party affiliation seek to ensure their incumbency by conferring benefits on their constituencies *now,* while deferring the costs, piling up massive deficits and mushrooming public debt to be paid by future generations. And, perhaps the most thoughtless and costly example of all is the pursuit of faster short-term economic growth without considering the longer-term consequences manifested in the degradation of the ecosystem that ultimately must sustain us all.

In an insightful article by James Hillman entitled *The Virtues of Caution,* he cites Aldous Huxley as observing that, as regards the original seven deadly sins, "…we moderns, despite our inventive genius and after so many centuries, have been able to add only one new sin. The sin? Haste… We live in the economics of hurry, and the planet itself heats up with the energy of our hastening." Perhaps then, we should pause and reflect on the long-run consequences we have wrought for ourselves and our posterity from our self-destructive short-term decision making, and take as our mantra that age-old caveat, *Haste makes waste…*

The Challenge of a Changing Paradigm
FEBRUARY, 2006

The furor over outsourcing, or "offshoring," is surely understandable. In a job market that has generated little real growth in wage and salary income in recent years, there is both anger and growing frustration among those manufacturing workers who have seen their jobs go elsewhere, or simply vanish in a relentless drive by employers to push their costs lower and lower. For increasing numbers of highly-skilled information technology workers, as well as other service workers whose skills have been replaced or displaced by digitalization, they, too, share that same anger and frustration. Despite their skills and their loyalty, neither of these traits any longer provides assurance of a decent paying job with some degree of permanence or security.

In the face of dramatic and ongoing increases in worker productivity that has allowed output to grow with far fewer workers, jobs once lost have become difficult to recoup. Given the spur to competitive pressures from globalization to cut costs, there is little doubt that the current angst over vanishing jobs is an augury of future concern as well. Like a concomitance of meteorological events that produce "the perfect storm," the ready availability of highly skilled workers around the world willing to accept far lower rates of compensation than U.S. workers, combined with the aforementioned gains in worker productivity and unrelenting pressure from global competition to pare costs, have produced a perfect storm of disillusionment and discontent among millions of American workers, even as the economy has grown.

A signal consequence of these forces has been a dramatic paradigm shift with which workers must now contend. The outgoing paradigm could be labeled "lifetime employment," in which hard-working, loyal employees could reasonably anticipate being rewarded with ongoing job security, subject only to the vicissitudes of cyclical unemployment from time to time. And, at retirement, that same worker could likely count on the prospect of a reasonably comfortable life, undergirded by a pension plan whose benefits were defined *and* honored by the employer. In its place, in growing ascendancy, is the paradigm that is best described as "lifetime employability." In the former paradigm, much of the burden of responsibility for assuring job and post-job security rested mainly on the shoulders of the employer. However, in the latter, it is the employee who bears most of the burden for her job security by making sure that she is capable of offering those skills the market may demand at any given moment, at whatever wage the global marketplace may dictate. This places a high premium on workers constantly anticipating and responding to the ever-changing needs of a globally competitive, fast-paced job market as they have become members of a giant global labor pool, where the requisite skill sets may be offered by foreign workers for far lower wages than those historically enjoyed by their American counterparts.

If further evidence of this changing paradigm were needed, one might take note of the recent announcements by IBM, Sprint, and other large corporations of a freeze in pension benefits for their employees, as well as outright repudiation of future pension obligations on the part of other major employers. Additionally, the ongoing shift from "defined benefit" plans to 401(k) "defined contribution" plans continues unabated, as more and more workers are coming to the realization that the security and comfort of their post-employment retirement years increasingly has come to depend upon themselves, and thus has become far more problematic. This is particularly true where high levels of indebtedness and meager personal saving rates are characteristic of so many workers and their families.

Even as the controversy rages as to whether or not outsourcing or offshoring is good for the American economy, there is a growing realization that, whatever may be the judgment over the relative merits of that phenomenon, the question itself is no longer relevant. Rather, the growing interconnectedness of the global economy has made it all but certain that outsourcing/offshoring is inevitable. Trade between nations is not likely to wane, and there is little solace, nor much economic sense, in reverting to a regime of protectionism that would surely invite retaliation. To be sure, there must be a basic element of fairness and reciprocity in all trade agreement to which we are a party. At the same time, the pace at which our workers may be displaced can and should be governed by our insistence upon trade agreements that embody appropriate safeguards for the rights of workers and for the environment, lest we stand aside and bear witness to a competitive "race to the bottom" for both working conditions and the integrity of the environment that sustains us.

The global economy is one in which competitive leadership is increasingly transient. Over the long haul, only ongoing investment in education and training, and in research and development that brings forth continuous innovation and a steady stream of desirable new offerings in the marketplace, can offer us the hope of a job market more insulated from competitive pressures from abroad. For many, the high and rising costs of securing an adequate and ongoing education presents a most formidable obstacle toward gaining and continually enhancing the skills they will need to compete. Clearly, the need to address the growing costs of higher education requires thoughtful deliberation and meaningful action, or else access to it may be beyond the grasp of growing numbers of our young people. At the same time, it may well be that a new public policy initiative is worthy of consideration. It would combine public service along with compensation earmarked for education, akin to the post-World War II G.I. Bill. Such an initiative could help make higher education and technical training more affordable, so that tomorrow's workers are not handicapped by a lack of the proper tools needed for tomorrow's job markets. As history has shown, such a public investment in human resources can bear enormous economic dividends to us as a nation.

Finally, there are those who may still find themselves left behind by the ever- changing winds of circumstance. For them, an assessment of our nation's unmet public needs in such areas as the infrastructure, the environment, healthcare, and homeland security among others, might offer ideas for both public and private investment to create productive and constructive job opportunities that would enhance human dignity, even as such initiatives further strengthen our economy. At a time when change has caused so much pain and disruption among those who seek nothing more than the dignity and security that comes from a decent job, it is incumbent upon us to think expansively and to act boldly in order to overcome the challenges posed by a changing paradigm.

Labor Day: So What's to Celebrate?
ALL SOULS FORUM • SEPTEMBER 2, 2007

I was thinking about the title that I gave to this presentation, Labor Day: So What's to Celebrate? If I chose, I could make this the shortest Forum to which you have ever been exposed, by simply saying in response to the question, "So what's to celebrate?" The answer would be: Not much.

In point of fact the record is mixed. But it is more accurate than not to say that from labor's point of view, there really isn't very much to celebrate. For most Americans, regrettably, Labor Day has become nothing more than just another day off. The roots of Labor Day going all the way back to 1882 have long since been forgotten by generations of American workers. Also forgotten are the roots of the very benefits and emoluments to which they are entitled as workers. They have no knowledge nor appreciation for the struggle that labor had to undergo in order to grasp and tear from management the very benefits so many workers today simply take for granted, and in most union representation elections, they vote against unions, recognizing that their benefits seem to be reasonably safe.

But if we were to have a short scorecard of what it is that we might wish to celebrate this Labor Day, let me give you a few suggestions on the plus side and on the minus side.

On the plus side: The minimum wage has just been raised, thanks to the Congress of the United States. After a ten-year hiatus at $5.15, Congress recently made the first of three incremental nudges upward to $5.85, on the road to a minimum wage in a couple of years of $7.10. The fact that it had been ten years during which there was no change in the minimum wage doesn't seem to have aroused very much passion, except among those workers who are minimum wage workers. And I suppose it's not inappropriate to point out that in that ten-year period, when workers at the minimum wage received no change, the members of Congress who legislate these sorts of things raised their own wages on ten separate occasions for a sum increase of about $33,000.

So the minimum wage went up. Let's cheer it. A census report was released last week with some "good news." The poverty level has declined for the second year in a row, down from 12.6 percent to 12.3 percent of the population. And, median family income for the first time in six years has risen. I'm going to come back to that census report because as is true with so much of economic statistics, there is less there than meets the eye.

Now, what can we say on the flip side of that ledger? What are some of the things that we have to deal with as we celebrate Labor Day in 2007? Well, at the federal level, there is no legal requirement in the United States for sick days or paid vacation days. It is true that on average American workers get about 10 vacation days. In Germany, that number is 27. In France, that number is 39. But I suspect that those American workers who are grateful for the 10 days that they have, few of them take those 10 days for fear that when they come back from that 10-day vacation, they may find a pink slip on their desk. And in the past decade or so, we have literally added more than a week of additional work time to America's working schedules.

Today as we contemplate Labor Day, one in four workers in this country earn less than $9 an hour in low-wage jobs. The Agriculture Department of the United States is the agency that determines what constitutes a poverty level of income. That poverty level of income is adjusted periodically. Right now it's at about $18,200 for a family of four. Now think about that for just a moment. You can do the math. On average, we work 2,000 hours a year. What would be the wage necessary to generate a poverty income? And what would that poverty income do for many people? The answer is, not very much. Besides the fact that the poverty level of income has long since been outdated in terms of the concept itself, because the Department of Agriculture, which came up with this measure, decided years ago that we would determine what constitutes a poverty level of income by taking a look at a family of four and determining how they allocated their budget. The Department of Agriculture determined that on average, one-third of that family budget should be allocated for food. And they took that number, multiplied it by three, and said, this constitutes the poverty level of income.

Now, the fact that food prices have risen and that therefore this measure automatically has risen, ought to be worth note. But the sad fact is that if you look at Americans' budgets these days, the biggest single item in that budget is the cost of shelter. And for many poor Americans, it is the inability for them to find reasonable shelter that puts them in a terribly difficult position. So the time has long since past when the poverty level should have been revised to reflect reality. And for those who say $18,200 is a lot more money than somebody earns in Africa or Latin America or Central America, I don't know with what contempt one ought to dismiss that argument on its face.

I said one in four workers earns less than $9 an hour. Fifty percent of American workers have one paid sick day. American workers now have received, thanks to the largesse of Congress, and the legislation that provides for unpaid family leave, a certain period when Americans may take some time off without pay to attend to the illnesses and the problems of family members. Unpaid family leave. That's the adjective that we have to remember.

The plight of American workers is a function of the relative state of the economy at any given moment, and, as a consequence, of longer-term developments that have shaped the background within which labor has to work. One of the most profound changes that the labor movement and workers have undergone in this country in recent years is a dramatic change from the concept of lifetime employment to the concept of lifetime employability.

Now let me explain the contrast between these. It was seldom the case, if ever, that any American worker ever enjoyed an ironclad contract in their place of employment that guaranteed them lifetime employment, that is to say, they took that job and they knew that they had a right to hold that job until they chose to retire at what was then the typical retirement age of 65 years, where they would get a gold watch and a luncheon and a pat on the back from the boss, and they would be able to retire with a pension plan that was more often than not a defined benefit plan. They knew what their pension rights entitled them to. They received these defined benefits as part of that labor relationship. I said no worker ever enjoyed that, except if you were a union worker in a written contract, and that written contract was revised as the term of the contract expired in every three years or four years.

But nonetheless, there was an understanding. If it was not a legal contract, it was understood to be a social contract, that in America, workers did their jobs and in return for doing a good job, they expected to be kept on board until they chose to retire, with periodic promotions and wage increases and the benefit package at the end of that road.

That time has long since past. Today American workers labor under the threat of employment-at-will. Without any reason whatsoever, the employer is free to terminate that employee at will.

In this new environment, we can change the notion of lifetime employment in which the place of employment, the organization, had an implied responsibility on its shoulders to take care of its workers. We now shift that responsibility almost entirely onto the backs of workers themselves, who are told that in this new environment of globalization, in this new environment where competition is not just down the street or around the corner, but literally from anyplace on the face of the earth, it is the responsibility of the employee to make sure at any given moment that they have those requisite skills that the job requires and that ensures their employability.

That is a very different environment, and in that environment, we have seen the spectacle of mass layoffs of highly paid workers who have found it very difficult if they've lost their employment at age 50 or 55 to ever get back into the labor force with a job at comparable wages and benefits. They have been unemployed for longer periods of time and more often than not, when they do find employment, it is at a considerably lower wage with few benefits.

That's the reality of work in America today. Workers who have a job are grateful for having that job, and they live under the constant of fear of being fired. That is the reason why one has seen a dramatic diminution in that segment of America's labor force that has been organized under union contracts. From a high point of about 33 to 35 percent of the American workforce, we are now looking at the private workforce enjoying a rate of union organization of about 8 percent. If you want to add government workers at local, state and federal levels into that mix, that bumps it up to about 12.5 percent. The fact is the labor union has lost sway even as the requirements of America's workers would suggest that never in our history has there been a greater need for union organization than right now. Companies in the United States are seeking to squeeze every last penny of profitability they can out of their workers. And the key to that profitability is either in increasing revenues, selling more of whatever it is they sell, or minimizing costs, and more often than not, minimizing costs means laying off workers.

The state of every American worker is not quite the same in this country. There was an article in *The Kansas City Star* entitled, "Money managers rake it in." You may recall John Edwards, who ran as a vice presidential candidate, spoke about two Americas. He talked about an America in which wages and emoluments keep rising, and another America in which more and more Americans are forced to struggle for their everyday existence.

This article, which talks about money managers, says a new report notes the huge pay disparity between executives and the people they employ. They looked at the average pay of leaders in different fields. In the United States Congress, the average pay is $171,200. In the military, the average pay for the hierarchy, for the leaders, is $178,542. Not too different. The federal government executive branch, the upper levels of the Social Security system—$198,369. C.E.O.s at nonprofit organizations—$965,698. These are nonprofit organizations. But the one that struck me is, what about the C.E.O.s of publicly traded companies in the United States? What is their average pay? $36.4 million. Compared with the average pay of American workers, that is simply 22,255 times as great.

When we talk about two Americas, there is a reality that we live in a society that more and more is characterized as separate and distinct from that which many people can identify with. Commentary by then-candidate for the United States Senate, Jim Webb, was right on. He said the most important and unfortunately the least debated issue in politics today is our society's steady drift toward a class-based system, the likes of which we have not seen since the 19th century. America's top tier has grown infinitely richer and more removed during the past 25 years. It is not unfair to say that they are literally living in a different country.

We cannot disentangle the welfare and the well-being of America's workers from the state of the American economy. We recently received a revised version of the Gross Domestic Product for the second quarter of this year (2007), and there was a great celebration about the fact that the numbers had been bumped up from an annual rate of increase of 3.4 percent to 4 percent. Obviously, an economy growing at 4 percent in many respects is better than an economy growing at 2 percent. And America's workers benefit when the economy is strong and healthy.

But the American economy these days is operating under a cloud. And that is a cloud brought on by the leaking of air out of a bubble that has grown in the real estate sector of the United States. Many of you in this room own your own homes. And if you bought those homes some years ago, you were able to sit back and watch the appreciation in the value of that particular home. Many of you looked at the appreciation of the value of that home and said, "Wow, I'm a lot richer than I used to be, and you know, we can add another room on to this house if we wish, or a deck, or put central air in, and so we will simply go to the bank that holds our mortgage, we're going to refinance the mortgage, cash out a chunk of that equity, and use that equity to pay for the improvements, or to buy a car, or to finance a vacation, or whatever we wish to do with it."

Countless numbers of Americans did that. And for many of those people, it worked out okay. Now more recently, housing prices have not only quit rising, they have in many parts of the country started to fall. For Americans who negotiated that fixed-rate mortgage, they're okay; they are still operating under the same rate of interest for that mortgage that they had previously. Many Americans at the lower end of the income spectrum in our socioeconomic setting under the best of circumstances would have been questionable borrowers. But did that stop the home mortgage industry from looking at poor Americans and saying, "Wow, this is an untapped market. Nobody has really paid very much attention to the sub-prime sector of the marketplace. Here's an opportunity for us to do well."

So what happened? These poorer Americans, like others, had aspirations to own a home. They were contacted by mortgage brokers. They were not terribly sophisticated, they were not terribly knowledgeable about what they were signing. They simply signed these papers on the promise that they were going to get a house. They were going to get a house with little or no down payment. They were going to get a house at a very low rate of interest. There would be substantial fees that the mortgage brokers would put into this contract, and they were not to worry about it. What happened was the home mortgage industry has changed very dramatically over the years.

For those of us who bought our houses 30 or 40 years ago, or even 20 years ago, the mortgage company that issued your home mortgage typically was associated with a savings and loan institution. They would do due diligence and make sure that you were creditworthy enough to buy that house, and typically the standard was, if your payments didn't exceed 25 percent of your annual income, that was a pretty good benchmark. They kept the mortgages in-house and serviced each for the life of the mortgage.

Now let's come back to these poorer Americans with questionable if not non-existing creditworthiness. They were duped into thinking that that teaser rate of interest they got might be the interest that would prevail during the life of the contract. But thanks to the invention of adjustable rate mortgages and variations on that theme, what they signed off on was an introductory rate of interest for the first year or two, after which time the rate would be re-set upward, and when the rate was re-set upward for many of these Americans, they found they could no longer afford the new monthly payments. And as that has occurred, many American homeowners have been forced into foreclosure. And foreclosures have been pressing on the market, because today's mortgage market doesn't look anything like the mortgage market of 20 or 30 or 40 years ago. Today, mortgage brokers have come into existence, independents, not necessarily bankers. They negotiate with a potential borrower. They lend them the money, issue the mortgage, and then that mortgage is immediately sold in the marketplace to someone who takes these mortgages and bundles them up into a big package that's called securitization. They bundle up the mortgages and convert those mortgages into a mortgage-backed security, or a mortgage-backed bond, which others are willing to pay for. And these mortgage-backed bonds are rated by rating agencies to assure that people know what it is they are buying. They are literally buying into a pool of home mortgages, some of which are very risky, some of which are very solid, and some in between.

Now, it sounds like this is an improvement that has helped many Americas who otherwise would not be able to get a house. But it really isn't, because in the process of issuing the mortgage, the mortgage broker, more often than not, with complicity on the part of the borrower, raised their earnings levels above that which the people were really earning. They falsified the earning statement. In addition, insofar as the loan was concerned, quite often they would employ appraisers who would appraise the property for a higher value than it really was worth, which meant that the amount that they lent was higher than the house was worth, simply giving them more interest that they would earn. The rating agencies, in turn, who should have known what was going on, either looked the other way or they themselves would rate these mortgage-backed securities that were not Triple A, the best rating, Triple A. And so on and on this process has gone, until the sub-prime mortgage market began to implode and more and more foreclosures have taken place.

Now, why do I harp on this? Because what happens in the housing industry in the United States is of inordinate importance to the well-being of the American economy and of the American worker. In the years 2001 through 2006, if you were to add up all of the dollars of economic growth that were occasioned during that period, fully 40 percent of that growth was attributable to the housing sector, to Americans either buying a house or refinancing their mortgages

Well, as I speak, between now and the end of 2008, approximately $850 billion in adjustable rate mortgages will be re-set at a higher rate. We are talking about a very sizable slice of the American population that is going to be affected by what we know is already in the pipeline. If we want to go out a little bit further, the sum total of existing adjustable rate mortgages that will have to be re-set from now beyond 2008 amounts to a trillion and a half dollars. We are looking at a veritable keg of dynamite that is getting ready to blow. And if the worst happens, if this market continues to implode as it is, and my own sense is that the decline in the housing sector has a long way to go before it ever reaches bottom, then the implications for the American economy and for America's job workers are very sobering indeed.

But before I stop, let me come back to what I gave you as a sense of good news earlier. Do you remember I referred to the Census report that indicated that average median family income had gone up, and the poverty level had gone down? The median household income was still, even having gone up, about a thousand dollars less than it was in the year 2000, which was the onset of the recession. What that means is that this is the first economic recovery that five years or more, almost six years after the recession hit bottom and the economy recovered, we were still below the earlier peak in average family median income.

I said that the poverty level has gone down. That's true, but that was very minuscule, and at the same time the poverty level has gone down, more and more Americans found themselves without any access to health insurance whatsoever in this country. So if one were to be honest about the state of America's workers and to ask, as we look forward to Labor Day, "What's to celebrate?", the answer is, not very much. American labor has lost dramatic ground in the last 10 to 15 years, ground that to my way of thinking is not likely to be readily made up in the foreseeable future. If we are to try to improve the lot of the poorest of the poor and the majority of America's workers, there are some things that absolutely must be done. And first and foremost, because this is a factor that relegates more people to poverty than any other, is the absence of health care for Americans. What this country needs, what is long overdue in this country, what we can afford, is universal health care.

At the same time access to health care is being denied to nearly 50 million Americans, the president will submit a supplemental request of the Congress for another $50 billion to fund the war in Iraq and Afghanistan That war is now costing America $3 billion every week. And we ought to reflect on the reality that when it comes to providing the most basic needs of Americans, the assurance that they can enjoy access to health care services if they need them, there doesn't seem to be enough money in this country. We can't afford that. But we can always seem to find money that we have to borrow to fight an ongoing war. That's something that you ought to sit down and try to explain to your children, whose sensibilities I think would be offended by that observation. Those same workers need to have offsets to job losses occasioned by globalization. The Trade Adjustment Assistance Act does provide for workers who get laid off because of foreign trade, to get some assistance. That law has to be amended to be far more generous.

And finally, if in fact the private sector of the American economy is now, in the year 2007, incapable of providing an adequate number of jobs to gainfully employ American citizens who have working skills, then we ought to harken back to 1933, when American and its government understood that the private economy was failing America's workers, and it was the obligation and responsibility of government to serve as employer of last resort. God knows how many bridges other than the one in the Twin Cities are ready to collapse, or how much public infrastructure is deteriorating under our feet.

Final comment: The first step on the road to any improvement in the plight of America's workers is a step that each of you in this room can take on that first Tuesday in November in 2008. Unless and until we change this government and the players in this government, to reflect a composition that is more concerned about the plight of average Americans, what I have said to you today in terms of the plight of America's workers is not going to change. So the first step is going to be taken with your feet, and if those feet don't lead into a polling place, don't blame it on anybody else.

Illegal Immigration: We Have Met the Enemy and It Is Us. But Who Is Us?

ALL SOULS FORUM • MAY 20, 2007

When I worked for the Federal Reserve system, to do any research project involved voluminous labor. You went to your librarian at the Fed. You would go through the files and look at the annotated bibliographies of the books that they had on a particular subject in which you were interested to see if some of them might be relevant. You would consult the Journal of Periodic Literature to see the array of articles on a particular subject. It was time-consuming. Today, in preparation for this presentation, I went on Google, and I said, "Okay, type in two words—illegal immigration—and see what happens."

As soon as I hit 'Go,' I got back 7,030,000 references to illegal immigration. And because I thought that somehow our foreign assistance programs also played a role in this particular subject, I searched the subject of U.S. foreign assistance on Google, and I came up with 19,000,000 hits. From this, I came to a conclusion that the subject of illegal immigration is highly contentious, highly complex, and highly voluminous, making anyone who represents themselves as an expert a fraud. Therefore, I would simply say to you, I did my duty. I came up with these reference sources. I direct your attention to them. Thank you and have a good life.

I wish it were that easy. But the fact is that it is a contentious and a complex subject. And if there are any in this audience who expect to go away satisfied that the position they hold on this subject is the correct position, I am afraid you're going to be terribly disappointed. Because it turns out that immigration, whether illegal or legal, is not a subject that is an unmitigated evil, nor is it an unmitigated good. For those who think that illegal immigration is harming America in some sense, I say to you the answer to that is yes. For those of you who feel that illegal immigration is benefiting the United States in some sense, I say to you similarly, the answer is yes. What we are looking for is a sense of perspective through which we can view this subject, because it is a subject that is not going to go away.

But let's talk a little bit about illegal immigration. I have come to the conclusion that we have met the enemy, and it is us. But who is us? Who exactly is guilty of fomenting illegal immigration?

Let's talk about some of the specifics regarding illegal immigration, some of the data. How many illegal immigrants are we talking about? Estimates range all over the place. The number that is most batted about is 12 million. Yet the estimates have been as low as 7 million and as high as 20 million. Where did these immigrants come from? Fifty-seven percent of them come from Mexico, 24 percent of them come from Central American and South American countries. Approximately 9 percent of them come from Asia, 6 percent from Europe and Canada, and the remainder from the rest of the world.

Well, how do people become illegal immigrants? There are basically three routes of illegal immigration. First, individuals can enter the United States by crossing the border without authorization or inspection. Second, they can come in to the United States under terms of legal entry, but they can violate those terms and stay and thus become an illegal immigrant. Or, they can stay beyond the authorized period for which their visa has allowed them entry into the United States.

Now, what are the causes of illegal immigration? If you were to say poverty is the root cause of illegal immigration, you wouldn't be too far off the mark. Illegal immigrants, particularly those coming from Mexico, have been portrayed as job seekers who sought good-paying job options in their own country, and finding none, did whatever was necessary to find gainful employment north of the border. So there are really two culprits here. One is poverty, and the second is the inability of the home country to provide gainful employment opportunities to their own citizens. And having said this, it should be equally obvious that if there is to be a solution to the problem of illegal immigration, part of that solution rests not with the United States, the country that has become the largest repository of illegal immigrants, but with those countries that have failed in their own economic polices to provide these poor people opportunity.

Is illegal immigration good for the country, or is not? Paul Samuelson, who is a Nobel Laureate in economics and an intellectual I admire greatly, says that there is no unitary, singular effect, good or bad, that arises from illegal immigration, but instead a variety of effects depending upon the economic class that you look at. What he means is that wealthier Americans tend to benefit from the illegal influx while poorer Americans suffer. Well, when you talk about wealthy Americans and poorer Americans, you are leaving out a very significant range of people in the middle. So, let me make this assertion, and that is, for those harboring concerns about illegal immigration, I would suggest you take a good look in the mirror and ask yourself if you bear some of the culpability for illegal immigration. Because after looking at all the data, the conclusion that I have reached is that illegal immigrants subsidize the lifestyles of many Americans well beyond the wealthiest. Ask yourself, for example, how much more would you be willing to pay, when you go to the produce department of the grocery store, for a head of lettuce, or a box of strawberries, or any of the seasonal fruits or vegetables that tend to be picked by stoop labor, primarily immigrants, many of whom are illegals. We rail about jobs being taken from Americans, but do we rail against the employers who knowingly employ illegal immigrants? Are we willing to enforce immigration laws as they relate to illegal immigration? The answer is no. When the Immigration and Naturalization Service was rolled into the Department of Homeland Security, there was a judgment that in order to enforce the border, it would require some 2,000 additional border guards. President Bush in his budget authorized 200 additional border guards. And it was only because of aggressive action on the part of the Congress of the United States that the number of new border guards increased by some 1,500.

So when you look at the economic impact, recognize there are disparate impacts, depending upon your own income position. But all of us who rail against illegal immigration but are unwilling to pursue employers who otherwise might have to pay higher wages, which translates into higher prices, are really not being truthful in terms of their concerns over this particular phenomenon.

I said that the fundamental cause of illegal immigration is the globalized shifts that have taken place in the workforce. It is poverty, to be sure, but poverty that has brought about a dramatic change in the nature of the global workforce. In our own country, what is becoming very clear is that our workforce is becoming more skilled at the same time the average age of our workforce is increasing. Now, what that means is workers are getting more educated and we no longer produce the workers in numbers required to do much of the unskilled work that is done and will continue to need to be done in our country. I am focusing on unskilled because it has been a long while since America's manufacturing prowess had to yield to the forces of globalization and the search for the bottom with employers moving their plants around the world in an effort to find the least cost of production.

Now, if there is a single statistic that might give you some insight into why illegal immigration has grown as a problem, think of this: In 1960, half of all American males dropped out of high school and became members of our unskilled labor force. That percentage has shrunk to 10 percent. The supply of available workers to do unskilled jobs has dropped by four-fifths. But do you think the demand for this kind of labor has dropped commensurate with the drop in supply? The answer is no. So what we have is an illegal immigration flow that is demand-driven, it is induced by our demands for goods and services in order to sustain the lifestyle we have chosen for ourselves.

We have quotas governing the number of immigrants who can come into this country legally. The problem is that the quotas and the nature of the demands for unskilled labor are out of sync. We have to change those quotas if we're serious about illegality. We have to change the quotas to reflect the realities of today's marketplace. Think of an American car manufacturer who requires a certain amount of steel to build the number of cars he can produce, but with a quota on the amount of steel that he can get that is only two-thirds of what he needs. We would agree it's an absurdity, to say, "Produce all the cars you want, but you can only get two-thirds of the steel you need." In the case of unskilled labor, in essence we're saying, "We like the lifestyle we've chosen, but we can't get the people who can sustain that lifestyle except through an illegal path." And that doesn't make any sense.

Ultimately, what we want is for immigrants to come to this country, but without the taint of illegality. We want to have the labor force that is necessary and beneficial to come here without fear of persecution for illegal entry. The suggestions that have been made to deal with the problem up to the very, very near past, have borne very little reality, and I would offer you some of the irrational paths that have been offered to address this problem.

Lou Dobbs is an interesting fellow. He is a consummate free-marketer, but when it comes to the issue of immigration, Lou Dobbs considers himself to be in the vanguard of those who say the solution is simple and that anybody who says its complex is just blowing smoke. What we need to do to deal with illegal immigration is to round up these illegal immigrants and deport them. Ship 'em back to their country. Lou is used to dealing in numbers but shrinks from offering an estimate as to what this would cost and how long this would take

Well, estimates have been made and assuming the unassumable, that we could in fact round these people up, the estimate is that it would probably take no less than five years to do the job, and it would cost $206 billion. That would be $40 billion dollars a year for five years to take care of deporting all these illegal immigrants. That is more than the annual budget for the Department of Homeland Security.

So, if you think the Lou Dobbs of the world have a monopoly on wisdom, go to the American taxpayer and say, "Hey, this is a good idea. Except we don't happen to have $206 billion in change at the moment."

Do you know that the border between the United States and Mexico, which provides for the greatest supply of illegals, is 1,954 miles long? Do you know that the Congress in its infinite wisdom, and President Bush, proposed that we build a fence, a 700-mile fence. You see, I have a problem. And the problem isn't that if you build a 40-foot fence, someone will build a 42-foot ladder. The problem isn't with the height of the fence. It is the length of the fence, and the absence of completeness. We know for a fact, don't we, that when there existed a wall between East Berlin and West Berlin, people were willing to risk death to escape from East to West in hopes for a better life. Is there anybody in this room who really believes that a 700-mile fence to guard a nearly 2,000 mile border is going to stop people who from desperation are seeking a better life for themselves and for their kids? I don't think so.

What can we do? I said the solution to this is not going to be found in terms of building fences, or pieces of legislation designed to provide legal avenues for citizenship or legal status. Those certainly are going to help. But as long as there exist incredible disparities in wealth and income around the world, America, with all its faults, will be seen as a beacon of opportunity for people. And America is going to have to accept the fact that illegal immigration will exist as long as countries that give rise to these huge numbers of illegal immigrants fail to provide opportunities for their own people.

So, foreign assistance, our trade policies, are going to play a role in this issue. If there is to be any hope for dealing with the issue of illegals, it's going to result from a collaborative global effort to assist nations to provide opportunities for their own citizens. And in this regard, the data are not terribly optimistic. The amount of foreign assistance that might be required is well in excess of what the United States foreign assistance funding has been in recent years. When it maxed out shortly after World War II with the Marshall Plan and the like, our foreign assistance amounted to approximately two percent of our gross domestic product. For your information, the United Nations has issued as a benchmark that nations ought to be giving foreign assistance at a rate of seven-tenths of one percent of their gross domestic product. The United States has a foreign assistance program that ranges between one-tenth of one percent and less than two-tenths of one percent of G.D.P.

And the issue is not simply the flow of dollars associated with that foreign assistance, but the nature of the assistance itself and the integrity of the governments that are the recipients. Too often, those foreign assistance dollars flow to governments that are innately corrupt. Their citizens see very few benefits. Paul Wolfowitz, who recently resigned from the World Bank, to his credit, viewed corruption as a major consideration in determining whether or not nations should receive foreign assistance funds. I think focusing on corruption was probably not a bad place to look, but the nature of what the World Bank over the years has done in terms of economic development programs, has tended to focus on the large showcase programs that more often than not typically reward U.S. corporations with the contracts to make those programs a reality. What we need are programs that provide employment for indigenous individuals in the poor countries. What we need are programs whose scale is more relevant to the needs of their societies, and there is an example that we can look to that to me suggests the possibility of some hope, and that's the growth of micro-lending initiatives.

Recently the gentleman who is credited with coming up with the idea of micro-lending was given a Nobel Peace Prize, and it was well-deserved. Micro-lending may help provide opportunities that otherwise would be foresworn for lack of monies. And when we talk about micro-lending and investment, what we're talking about in the case of many of these poor people, are miniscule sums of money that make dramatic differences in their lives and their hopes for the future.

Let me introduce something that ought to raise the level of urgency. A report recently was issued by CNA Corporation. I believe CNA is an acronym for the Center for Naval Analysis, which in Cold War days, used to do research on military issues. But they recently issued a report, the title of which was National Security and the Threat of Climate Change. Now you may ask yourself, what does this have to do with illegal immigration?

Well, let me share with you one of the conclusions they reached. They accept the validity of the forecasts regarding global warming and its consequences, and they say such changes will add significantly to existing tensions and may facilitate weakened governance, economic collapses, human migrations, and potential conflicts.

Now, reflect on this fact: Approximately two-thirds of the world's inhabitants live near a coastline. Thus, with global warming and rising sea levels, we might see flooding of low-lying coastal lands that could lead to massive migrations of people, the scale of which makes our illegal immigration problem pale in significance. We're talking about the possibility of upwards of one billion of the world's people being displaced by the consequences of climate change and adding to the pressures on national economies that are already stemming from illegal immigration.

I have barely touched the surface of this subject, and when I said at the very outset that perhaps the most prudent thing for me to do would be simply say, call on Google and type in illegal immigration, and take the rest of your life to scroll through those 7,030,000 reference sources, I wasn't far off the mark. We have had forums on this subject that have been matters of considerable contention and conflict among well-meaning people. Those conflicts will not go away. I hope my presentation at least has illuminated some of the data and some of the considerations we must bear in mind as we try to address what, for practical purposes, seems to be to me an interminably intractable issue.

Section Two:
Learning From History
Economic Analysis

The Surprising Economy
DECEMBER, 2005

The recent past has borne witness to a series of destructive and disruptive Gulf Coast hurricanes, dramatically rising energy costs and a continued rise in interest rates that has prompted some visible softening in the housing market, among other factors that should have slowed the economy. Nonetheless, as in the old Timex watch commercial, the American economy appears to have managed to "take a licking and keep on ticking." Upward revised estimates of the third quarter Gross Domestic Product (GDP), and robust employment gains in November following two earlier months of lackluster job growth, seem to be indicative of an economy with a significant amount of resilience in the face of adversity. Expectations that the economy would exhibit serious adverse effects on the rate of growth owing to the aforementioned factors were not borne out by the GDP data for the July-September period. Indeed, the preliminary estimate of third quarter GDP growth at an annual rate of 3.8 percent was a half point higher than that of the preceding quarter. And the revised estimate for GDP of 4.3 percent was a full point higher, exceeding the "guesstimates" of most business forecasters, and was the strongest quarterly performance in more than as year and a half.

Is the economy really as vibrant as it appears to be? Or is the economy's capacity for generating ongoing favorable surprises likely to succumb to factors that are inimical to a continued high rate of growth? A closer look at some of the data may help to shed some light on the answers.

In disaggregating the GDP data, it certainly appears as though the strength of the economy was more real than illusory. Spending by both consumers and businesses was strong. After revision, third quarter consumer spending was boosted upward from an annual rate of 3.9 percent to 4.2 percent. This was the best performance by consumers since the final quarter of 2004. At the same time, bolstered by healthy corporate profits over the past several years, business spending for capital equipment and software in the quarter registered a healthy gain at an annual rate of 10.8 percent, revised upward from a preliminary estimate of 8.9 percent. In addition, although the housing sector failed to exceed the nearly 11 percent rate of investment spending in the second quarter of the year, nonetheless it was revised upward sharply from the preliminary estimate of 4.8 percent growth to a more robust gain of 8.4 percent. Additionally, the pace of economic activity in the third quarter did not seem to trigger any obvious inflationary pressures. The quarterly GDP Price Deflator rose at an annual rate of 3.6 percent, a tad below initial estimates. However, the "core" rate of inflation, which excludes the highly volatile food and energy components, rose by only 1.2 percent, well below the 1.7 percent increase in the preceding quarter.

As noted earlier, the good news on the economy's third quarter performance was amplified by the most recent labor market release for November. Owing to the disruptions caused by Hurricane Katrina, total employment in September, not unexpectedly, fell for the first time in two years. And in October, the employment gain was a very weak 56,000. Thus, the November release was awaited with considerable anticipation. It did not prove disappointing. Non-farm payroll employment in November increased by 215,000, the biggest monthly gain since July. Gains were widespread across industries, with construction adding nearly 40,000 jobs, and manufacturing adding 11,000 new workers. Whether this is an augury of a strong labor market remains to be seen, but other economic data subsequent to September suggest that developments in the economy would be supportive of further job gains in the months ahead.

The spike in prices at the gasoline pump that saw the price per gallon rise above $3 has retreated significantly, and is now about $1 a gallon less than at its peak. This has buoyed consumer confidence and improved the prospects for stronger year-end retail sales. In October, before the retreat in gas prices had fully been manifested, the Commerce Department reported that retail sales fell by 0.1 percent, dragged down by a drop in auto sales of more than 3.5 percent. Still, the drop was much less than the 0.7 percent decline that was expected by most analysts. And, when auto sales losses are excluded, retail sales for the month rose by nearly a full percentage point. Sales gains were especially evident in specialty clothing stores, as well as department stores. When combined with anecdotal evidence indicative of a strong start to the traditional holiday sales season, it appears as though consumers may have shed their cautiousness. An added positive sign was the resurgence in industrial production in October. After a fall of 1.5 percent in September, the biggest monthly drop in production in over two decades, the Industrial Production Index rose in October by nearly a full percent, as hurricane- damaged facilities in the Gulf were brought back on line. Additional evidence of strength in October came from a very sizable increase in orders for durable goods, particularly for aircraft, as well as record sales of new homes that came in the face of reports that suggest this key sector is showing signs of slowing. All in all, it appears as though the economy still has considerable forward momentum as the year draws to a close, and ongoing reconstruction efforts in the Gulf Coast states will surely add to that. But can this momentum be sustained throughout 2006 and beyond?

The economic optimist tends to view a glass as "half-full." The pessimist would say with equal accuracy that the same glass is "half-empty." The cautionary economist might well eschew passing judgment on the level in the glass, and reflect on what, if any hazards to sustained, strong economic growth should be given consideration before passing judgment on the future. For example, the retreat in gasoline prices should not blind one to the fact that prices are still a good deal higher at year-end then they were a year ago. Furthermore, the real squeeze from heightened energy prices will be more fully demonstrated when Americans get their next monthly utility bills. If consumers had significant levels of discretionary income in hand, this would not necessarily detract from their ability to "shop 'til they drop." But, this is surely not the case for large numbers of people. For, despite modest inflation, the growth in the overall economy since late 2001 when the economic recovery began has failed to raise real family incomes. Economist Paul Krugman, writing in *The New York Times* of December 5th, observed:

> "Behind the disconnect between economic growth and family incomes, lies the extremely lopsided nature of the economic recovery that began in late 2001. The growth in corporate profits has…been spectacular. Even after adjusting for inflation, profits have risen more than 50 percent since the last quarter of But real wage and salary income is up less than 7 percent."

As disposable income from wage and salary earnings has lagged behind the growth in consumer spending, more and more consumers have either drawn down their savings or relied upon increased debt to make up the difference. After a drop in the saving rate in July to a negative 0.6 percent, in August the personal saving rate fell to a post-Depression low of 2.2 percent, and remains negative for the fourth straight month at this writing. As a consequence, households have been forced to devote record amounts of their disposable income simply to service their outstanding debt, even as banks report rising levels of defaults.

For many other Americans, their homes have not simply been their "castles." They have, in effect, become their "banks" as well, as the combination of housing price inflation with historically low mortgage rates prompted refinancing activities and cashouts that served to fuel spending. However, even after acknowledging record new-home sales in October, there are growing signs that the housing sector is growing less buoyant. The inventory of unsold homes has grown and those houses remain on the market for longer periods of time. On the heels of persistent increases in short-term interest rates by the Federal Reserve, mortgage rates have risen and housing price inflation has slowed, and the number of refinancings has diminished in turn. Thus, for more and more people, continued high levels of spending are becoming more problematic. Given the critical importance of the consumer to overall economic growth and the extraordinary extent to which the housing sector directly and indirectly has fueled consumer spending since 2000, the mounting evidence of a slowdown in the housing market, and its implications for continued high levels of consumer spending, must be viewed as a source of concern and a potential hazard to future growth.

Other legitimate areas of concern include an auto sector that appears to lack the ability to provide the level of stimulus to the economy that it did earlier. Recently, both Ford and General Motors have announced further plant closings and layoffs. Downsizing and outsourcing continues across a range of industries, and employers are demanding significant "givebacks" from their workers, adding further strain on already stretched family incomes. On the fiscal front, the stimulus to the economy from increased governmental spending on Gulf Coast reconstruction and the war in Iraq/Afghanistan must be counterbalanced by a growing uneasiness over a Federal budget deficit that has grown enormously over the past several years. Certainly, outgoing Fed Chairman Alan Greenspan has made public his concern. And, incoming Fed Chairman Bernanke, given his anti-inflation bias, is unlikely to dramatically reverse Fed policy in the face of an economy that seemingly remains poised for further growth. To this mix one should add the presence of an "800 lb. gorilla" in the form of a foreign trade deficit approaching $800 billion. Our ability to sustain such a deficit over time depends upon the continued willingness of our major trading partners to finance it at interest rates that they continue to find sufficiently attractive. Thus, from both the Federal budget deficit and the trade deficit, the implications for higher interest rates should be apparent. The overall economy has not yet slowed as interest rates have risen. But, over time, as past experience has amply demonstrated, the restraining effects of progressively higher interest rates do work their way through the economy. As already noted, higher mortgage rates are slowing the housing sector. Refinancing has lost a good deal of its attractiveness as a source of funding consumer expenditures. With debt service requirements now accounting for a record 13.6 percent of disposable income, future consumer spending is becoming increasingly vulnerable to higher interest rates.

As noted at the outset, the economy has been surprisingly resilient in the face of adversity. A large measure of that resilience has been a function of a very strong housing market and the positive spillovers from that market served to undergird strong spending by consumers. That favorable confluence of events is giving way to growing uncertainty in an environment in which the financial reserves of many households are virtually non-existent. The ability of the economy to continue to generate favorable surprises is not unlimited. In the future, it will have to contend with a growing likelihood that the public policy environment that was supportive of strong economic growth will give way to one that is more restrictive. If that should be the case, we may well find that the next economic surprise will be far less welcome than its predecessor.

On Learning From History
SEPTEMBER, 2007

*Those who do not read history are doomed to repeat it.
Those who fail to learn from the mistakes of their predecessors
are destined to repeat them.*
—GEORGE SANTAYANA

The current upheaval in the sub-prime mortgage market, and in credit and financial markets more generally, has revealed at its source an admixture of factors responsible for its onset and burgeoning growth. In recent weeks and months, as the "collateral damage" from the meltdown in the sub-prime sector has spread, sweeping aside earlier denials by such luminaries as Treasury Secretary Henry Paulson that the problems emanating from it were "largely contained," it has provided numerous opportunities for observers in the business and financial world to pen colorful prose to describe what is going on.

For example, in an article entitled *Not So Smart,* in the September 3 edition of *Business Week,* the authors lead with this observation, "In an era of easy money, the pros forgot that the party can't last forever."

The problems began with the understandable aspirations to become homeowners of countless numbers of borrowers of suspect, if not altogether weak creditworthiness. If these borrowers were unsophisticated or uninformed when it came to questioning the seemingly attractive mortgage loan packages that were being put before them, it seems clear that the lenders should have been well aware of the high risks associated with many of these loans. But the lure of high rates of return clouded their judgment. In trying to make some sense of what seems to be the utter suspension of due diligence, the *Business Week* article offers its readers a road map that encapsulates the process at work.

> "…One good place to start: the ways various financial players indulged in layer upon layer of leverage, much of it far from transparent. Mortgage lenders threw out common sense underwriting standards. Wall Street sliced and diced the loans, creating the illusion that risk somehow disappeared in the process. Hedge funds then multiplied the leverage by borrowing copiously to buy securities based upon the rearranged mortgages. In their version of the game, private equity firms used loads of debt to launch unprecedented buyouts."

Thus, the image of an endless party was built upon a shaky foundation that had as its prime ingredients the magical powers of securitization and leverage. Not only had mortgage lenders managed to come up with a variety of creative mortgage options with numerous fees and punitive pre-payment penalties; they also required little or no down payment, with very low introductory "teaser" rates of interest, and great flexibility for borrowers on interest and/or principal payments. At the same time, and unlike mortgage lending practices of earlier years, the lenders would seldom retain and service the loans they had made. Rather, they would quickly sell them to other investors to be bundled or "securitized" into mortgage-backed bonds that would then find their way into the portfolios of other financial institutions, pension funds and investors with varying degrees of risk tolerance. At this point, as purchasers of these securities would find to their dismay, we can add the element of mendacity to the mix of factors that have led to this current calamity. It should be remembered that a significant contributory factor that fueled the stock bubble of the 1990s, and that resulted in a crash late in the decade, was the culpability of accountants who signed off on grossly overstated corporate earning statements. In the case of the current unwinding of the real estate bubble, rating agencies must bear a large share of blame for having exaggerated the investment quality of the mortgage-backed securities that have been a prominent feature of the current debacle.

As long as interest rates remained low and real estate prices continued to rise, even the shakiest of this newly-minted class of homeowners might be able to meet the monthly payments and so hang on to their homes. However, when the air began to seep out of the housing bubble and interest rates on adjustable rate mortgages were reset upward, the real-world consequences of this shaky pyramid would become manifest in growing foreclosures, first among sub-prime borrowers, with the adverse financial waves rippling out ever more widely in the marketplace among the various players. A hint of the magnitude of what still may lie ahead may be seen in a commentary, *Mortgage Mayhem,* found in *Fortune* magazine of September 3. The authors note, "Home-loan default rates—especially for subprime loans—have nearly tripled since 2006. There's no end in sight: Adjustable-rate loans worth $850 billion are scheduled to reset by 2008. That will require borrowers to make larger payments, pushing defaults even higher." And, as Michael Greenberger, former director of the Commodity Futures Trading Commission commented in *Business Week,* "…we don't yet know the full extent of the complex borrowing arrangements on which the recent boom was built. There's embedded leverage all over the place, and no one knows how far it goes in the system. …There's billions and billions of dollars racing around the economy that no one can track."

The *Business Week* article noted at the outset did offer an insight into the hubris of some of the participants in what seemed to them to be a "sure thing":

> "The boasting and the bluster that marked the just-ended era of easy money varied depending on the speaker and his stake in the boom. But the underlying message was consistent: This time it's different. When it came to the hazards associated with borrowing, the old rules no longer applied. …The titans of home loans announced they had perfected software that could spit out interest rates and fee structures for even the least reliable of buyers. The algorithms, they claimed, couldn't fail."

It might be wise, in the presence of those who preach the gospel of risk-free gain in perpetuity, to hang on to your wallet tightly with both hands. Not only did they lack any doubt as to the certainty of the outcome, it was equally clear that humility was not readily visible as a sign of character among this "smart money" crowd. It would seem equally doubtful that many among them were avid students of history and/or appreciative of its lessons. It must also be said that, although the housing boom did allow many abuses to be perpetrated by opportunists, it was also the case that many homeowners, by means of refinancing, were able prudently to put a portion of the appreciated equity in their homes to constructive uses without compromising their overall financial wellbeing.

Perhaps it is simply a function of one's age and the passage of years that should give us some pause to reflect on what many have brought upon themselves in their relentless drive to squeeze every last dollar of profit from their exertions. Many, if not most of the readers of this essay can remember a time, not so long ago, when our lives seemed less hurried and harried. Home mortgage loans were largely the province of savings and loan entities and they originated and kept those loans "in-house," with most of the mortgages specifying a fixed rate of interest for the duration of the loan. To be sure, down payments were required and one's creditworthiness had to be assured. People tended to regard saving as virtuous and piling on indebtedness in order to satisfy the desire for instant gratification was indulged in by far fewer people than is the case today. Today's home-equity loans were referred to then as "second-mortgages," and one did not regard them as affording us bragging rights for having procured one. The richness of our lives was not necessarily defined in terms of our net worth or the volume of "stuff" we had managed to accumulate over the years. Still, whatever might have been the shortfalls of such a time insofar as material things might have been concerned; it did nonetheless offer us a gentler pace of life with friends and family, and an alternative to the unrelenting "getting and seeking" that is so characteristic of our current existence.

It is to be hoped that, from the pain and the travails we are presently undergoing and that almost certainly still lie ahead of us, we might read this history well so that we are not doomed to repeat it.

About That 800 Pound Gorilla
JUNE, 2006

Many of us are familiar with the conundrum posed by having an 800 pound gorilla walk into a bar. To the question, "Where does an 800 pound gorilla sit?" the answer is readily forthcoming; "anywhere he wants." I was reminded of this old joke by an article I read recently in the April 24 *Business Week, The Runaway Trade Giant.* As one might suspect, the article dealt with the Peoples Republic of China, and its overall theme was struck in the introductory observation that, "…As its impact on the U.S. economy expands, China is also growing less vulnerable to American pressure on key issues."

What we have discovered, increasingly to our chagrin, is that the mythical 800 pound gorilla has in reality turned out to be a very formidable Chinese dragon. With each passing day, its economic might grows, as do the implications and uncertainties for our own economy and its wellbeing. Perhaps, as a back-handed compliment to the abandonment by the Chinese of any ideological economic constraints, their growth has been a testament to the practical consequences of a titular Communist nation having adopted the Capitalist paradigm as the driver of their economic fortune. In its wake, the economy has performed as though it were "on steroids," creating a vast consumer-based middle class, even as it has relegated the poorest of its poor peasant class to a hardscrabble life. Whether the emergence of a growing middle class with access to the outside world via the Internet with knowledge of "how the other half lives," will serve as the "irresistible force" that meets and overwhelms the "immovable object" in the form of a Communist system of governance, remains to be seen.

What is not really subject to dispute is that wherever the economic presence of the Peoples Republic of China has made itself felt, its presence is moving others aside in jockeying for a place at the head of the global economic table. The recent state visit of President Hu Jintao, and the velvet glove treatment afforded to him by our government was indicative of the major player status that China has attained. Although President Hu returned to China with a shopping bag filled with Boeing jet planes, as well as a variety of other American goods, the shopping spree though certainly welcome will not materially affect our badly skewed and adverse trade balance with China. The U.S. trade deficit with China in the year 2000 amounted to about $80 billion; by 2005 that deficit had swelled to approximately $200 billion. Neither did the exchange of pleasantries between our two countries move us further toward resolution of such longstanding complaints on our part with regard to the exchange rate of the yuan vis-à-vis the U. S. dollar, as well as piracy of intellectual properties and allegations of dumping or inappropriate use of subsidies by the Chinese to favor their domestic producers. One might well ask why the United States has been unable to ameliorate the situation, or to punish China for a host of impediments to a more equitable trading balance between our two countries.

Surely among those factors that militate towards restraint on our part is the sheer exhilaration that comes from savoring growing access to a market of 1.3 billion people, particularly in the light of the spectacular and ongoing growth of a burgeoning middle class of consumers. Indeed, recent articles on the subject have made the point that the Chinese government is encouraging its populace to cut back on their tight-fisted saving habit and to spend more freely. As welcome as such efforts may be, it remains the case that most of their spending is on such domestic necessities as housing, education and healthcare. In addition, many of the consumer goods they purchase, while made by American companies, are in fact produced by Chinese subsidiaries of those same firms and therefore do not serve to reduce our trade imbalance. Nonetheless, with such a big stake for these companies to share in such a huge market, and with their overseas investments accounting for a growing share of their profitability, American companies are loathe to be overly critical of China for fear of compromising a potentially more expanded set of future opportunities. In addition, as a prime beneficiary of America's outsourcing of much of our manufacturing base, many American firms have become hooked on the "China fix" of inordinately low wages that beef up their bottom lines. Like all such addictions, once hooked, it is very difficult to change without considerable adjustment pains.

But perhaps a more persuasive and invidious reason for our inability to domesticate China's push towards the head of the table has more to do with our own bad habits, rather than those of China. As perhaps the most "conspicuous consumers" on earth, we have an apparently insatiable appetite for "things," many of which increasingly are coming from China, thus contributing to the enormous trade deficit. While it is true that much of our private consumption is being accommodated by dipping ever deeply into debt by hard-pressed American consumers, it is also true that the fiscal condition of the United States is equally reflective of a country that is living far beyond its means. In short, our government is spending far more than it is taking in on the revenue side, creating a huge public deficit that must be financed by borrowing upwards of $2 billion per day. The trading partners with whom we have amassed our sizable trade deficits have, in turn, become the recipients of significant surpluses of funds. These same countries, which of course include China, have in reality become our creditors by reinvesting their excess funds in a variety of dollar-denominated financial assets both public and private. Thus, we have become increasingly dependent on them to sustain our profligate ways. To disturb this relationship could precipitate a flight from dollar investments elsewhere, with a consequent drop in the value of the U.S. dollar as well as a run up in interest rates that would surely have an adverse impact on our economy.

If this set of circumstances does not trigger at least a modicum of concern on our part, the dramatic run up in energy prices should offer added pause for reflection. Not only must we be mindful of our debtor status with China, at the same time, our country and China are butting heads around the world as we seek to reinforce or establish our accessibility to a shrinking pool of hydrocarbons and/or other increasingly scarce vital natural resources. And, we have little if any leverage that we might exert on our giant competitor that would afford us the ability to leap past them to the head of the line. With the prospect of high energy prices as far into the future as the eye can see, and in the absence of any serious efforts at improving our fiscal situation, there is little hope that we may shrink either of the twin deficits that have made our country hostage to the good will of those who daily extend credit to us. In this regard, we should not count on China to radically alter its way of doing business with us to our advantage. For, as Shakespeare observed in his play, *Julius Caesar,* "…The fault dear Brutus is not in our stars, but in ourselves that we are underlings." Apropos, the *Business Week* article to which I referred at the outset closed with this relevant thought:

> "What can be done to achieve radical change? You will not litigate a country into changing its more important principles on how to run its economy. …China the heavyweight will set the rules for some time to come."

For the foreseeable future then, it would appear as though we should get used to that 800 pound gorilla sitting any where he chooses.

Economic Theories
JOHNSON COUNTY COMMUNITY COLLEGE
JANUARY 24, 1993

It's important to clear up some confusion with respect to three different systems that frequently get confused: capitalism, socialism, and communism. Economies can be organized in a variety of different ways, but they all have to address the same questions, quite simply, what does the economy produce, the nature of the array of goods and services that it produces, how does it pull together the resources in order to produce those goods and services, and finally, how does one distribute the fruits of that production. Whether one calls itself a capitalist or free market system, or a socialist system, or a communist system, the relative success or failure in dealing with those considerations is an appropriate judgment on how well that system has performed.

I'm not talking about a political system. I'm talking about an economic system. The terms tend to be confused. When I was an undergraduate student, I came across a very thin monograph written by even then a not-so-obscure professor of economics at the University of Chicago, Milton Friedman, and it was entitled *Capitalism and Freedom*. Capitalism and freedom. Suffice it to say that if one read the book, one was forced to conclude that only a capitalist system was consistent with freedom. And I think it is that sense of confusion that in the minds of an awful lot of people still exists.

So the first order of business is to dispel the notion that freedom is consistent only with a market system. All you have to do is look at the Scandinavian countries to recognize that there are elements of socialism present in those particular countries. There are elements of socialism present in Great Britain, and there are even elements of socialism present in the United States of America.

Now, what do we mean by capitalism, what do we mean by socialism, what do we mean by communism? I am not here talking about democracy, dictatorship, authoritarianism, which are different forms of governmental organization with varying degrees of freedom. I am talking about economic systems.

What are the touchstones of a capitalist or market system? It is a system in which individuals own private property and in which the material means of production are in the hands of private individuals for the most part. It is a system in which resources respond to signals that come from the market between buyers and sellers, and in which the outcome is largely determined by voluntary actions between buyers and sellers.

If capitalism represents largely private ownership and operation of the means of production, then you can define socialism by saying it is government ownership and operation of the means of production. In the United States, the Tennessee Valley Authority is as clear a socialist enterprise as anything I know. It was put together for the sole purpose of providing power to a portion of the country that didn't have it. It is owned and operated by the United States Government.

Under a socialist system, there can be varying degrees of market signaling. The fact that the government owns the means of production doesn't mean that they may or may not rely upon the market to provide them with signals to direct the use of their resources. And the farther they move away from market signaling and the greater the overall degree of government involvement in the operation of the economy, the closer it becomes to a centrally planned or centrally controlled socialist economy, such as that of the former Soviet Union.

Finally, what is communism? I am not sure that we have very many operative examples of communism around. I think at its outset perhaps the kibbutz system in Israel would have been an example of communism. Communism was a system in which government was going to wither away and the individual would have evolved to the point that the system would have been guided by a rather simple maxim: From each according to his or her ability, to each according to his or her needs. Perhaps in an environment in which the individuals have become perfected, such a system could operate. But in the world in which we live, there are very, very few examples of such an operative system.

There are countries that have a significant degree of ownership and operation of their means of production by government which are democratic countries in which this organization has been arrived at by a consensus of the elected. There are also countries, such as the former Soviet Union, in which socialism came into being as a consequence of revolution and nobody voted on the distribution of those resources, they were simply taken over by the state and operated by the state.

But where is the socialist paradigm today, and where is it going? I would say it's down but not out. There are momentous changes occurring around the world today. The most momentous have not occurred within the economic sphere, but within the political sphere. These are countries that have struggled under an authoritarian form of government for a long time that are beginning to espouse the tenets of democracy and put in place democratic forms of government. But the prospects for democracy are a function of the ability of the economic system to provide at least some decent standard of living. In short, the political experiment in Russia is dependant upon the extent to which the economic transition that is presently underway is or is not successful. In the final analysis, hungry people are not going to vote for democracy if the alternative to democracy promises them bread.

Yesterday in the paper, there was a very brief item entitled "Passages," and it's one of the great ironies:

> "Deng Xiaoping urged China to continue his economic reforms. Deng cited the growth under his capitalist-style reforms, saying, 'I hope you will not lose the opportunities for progress. For China the opportunities for great development are not many.'"

It's extraordinary that this is coming from the leader of the last giant communist nation on earth. And what in effect is he saying? Let us continue down the path to greater liberalization of our economy, because therein lies the best hope for a better life for our people. Now my own sense is that the likelihood of successful economic reform is greater in China than it is in the former Soviet Union. And I think that a corollary of successful economic reform will be a gradual political reform within China.

I see in China an extraordinary situation emerging. While they are still paying considerable lip service to socialism, much of the real action in terms of more dynamic growth and increased freedom of initiative, is taking place where economic reforms allow a greater sense of market participation.

Now, counter that to what is taking place in the former Soviet Union. Even before the total breakup of the Soviet Union, the three Baltic states were in the vanguard of pleading for their independence—Lithuania, Latvia, and Estonia. Now, some weeks ago, Lithuania just reelected the former communist government that it threw out when it obtained its independence.

Why? Because Lithuania, while it sought independence from the Soviet Union, also sought a better way of life, a higher standard of living. To the extent that they have been unsuccessful in making a rapid transition from a socialist, centrally planned system to a more market-oriented system, they have seen a tremendous amount of disruption, a tremendous amount of pain, and have not yet realized the fruits of independence or freedom. So, when promised a return to greater stability and less insecurity, that's precisely what they voted for. And therein lies the lesson. For those of us who are concerned about the evolution of political democracy, we have to be equally concerned about the evolution of economic systems towards those kinds of institutions that provide for their people a better way of life. While it is clear that the Soviet system of economics was a dismal failure, if you were to ask many of the citizens of the former Soviet Union whether they are more content today as opposed to what they had, there would be a certain yearning for the past. And that's extremely dangerous for the future of political democracy in this world.

The transition from an economy that is centrally planned to one in which one allows private ownership and all that that implies—the volatility and insecurities that accompany business cycles, inequalities in income distribution, wide gaps between rich and poor—is a system which is really quite alien to people in Eastern Europe. And what we have seen in the initial stages of economic reform within Eastern Europe and certainly within Russia, is an enormous amount of resentment at the inability for one's wages to cover the fundamentals which formerly were accommodated by those wages; at the growing appearance of a distinct class within society that is earning significantly more than the rest of society.

What is the best approach to realizing political democracy, is it to put political democracy before economic freedom, or is to put greater economic freedom before political democracy? The Chinese example would suggest that that the latter seems to be the more intelligent approach; that raising the well-being of the lot of the people is an absolutely indispensable precondition for creating the kind of ground within which democratic political institutions can take root. And unless that ground has been prepared by tangible and visible progress in economics, the prognosis for successful transplantation of political institutions into that soil is very, very poor.

The history of economic systems suggests, with a reasonable degree of persuasiveness, that those systems that afford to individuals a greater degree of freedom and a greater degree of opportunity to profit by their own initiative, a greater degree of opportunity to own property, probably stand a greater likelihood of success in moving the economy to a higher level of living.

If you reflect on the increasing globalization that is taking place, then you have to come to one inescapable conclusion: Only those economies that do the best job of allocating their resources, only those economies that do the best job of producing the very best goods and services of the highest quality at the lowest relative prices, are going to enjoy any measure of success and survivability.

Now, that is a world in which economic forces can be very cruel for the participants. We have watched a very significant transplantation of many American industries to countries where the cost of labor is significantly less. An open world market economy is an economy that is full of challenges.

Those challenges can better be met by a market system. If you're dealing with a relatively closed economic system in which the wants of the citizens are relatively few, then it's quite possible to address those within a closed system by having a highly regulated and centralized economy. And in fact, before the communist government was in place in China, starvation was ever-present in China. They had markets, they had ownership of private property. Following the revolution, that all disappeared. But with an authoritarian government and a socialist-communist economy, they were able to do remarkable things with respect to the provision of certain basic considerations that their citizens had never enjoyed. And it is for that reason that the government was able to survive during that period.

But as that system has evolved into one in which the citizen now can look out on a world and see that other people have yet more than they, and they can aspire to yet more, the system grows increasingly incapable of addressing that greater complexity and diversity of needs, and that's why

Deng Xiaoping and the economic reformers have come to recognize the virtues of allowing greater flexibility into that system.

So 20 years from now, certainly 10 years from now, within the People's Republic of China, you will see continued progress toward an economy with freer, more market-oriented institutions. Whether or not that same transformation will take place within Eastern Europe is an open question at this point. Certainly within some countries—Poland, Hungary—there is evidence of successful movements towards a more market-oriented economy. But within the former Soviet Union, there is an awful lot of instability and friction and controversy that has not yet allowed us to reach a firm and unequivocal conclusion regarding the prospects either for economic reform or for political democracy.

The stakes in this transformation process are very, very high. Absent political reform, or absent economic reform that is satisfactory to its citizens, these democratic shoots that have taken root in Eastern Europe are liable to wither and die.

I don't argue that a market system is a perfect system for all countries. But I would suggest to you that a market system such as we have in the United States, in an environment that has a reasonably rich tradition of political democracy that is responsive to the concerns of its citizens, probably represents the best combination that humankind can aspire to. And so given that notion, I would suggest that while socialism is down but not yet out for the count, I would bet against the evolution of socialism as a way of doing business in this world.

The Economy:
Is the Glass Half Full or Half Empty?
ALL SOULS FORUM • SEPTEMBER 11, 1994

How can one make the assertion that at the same time the glass is indeed both half full and half empty? In the half-full sense, the period of economic growth has now been sustained for more than 13 consecutive quarters, which makes it a mature expansion. And the longer these business-cycle expansions go on, the more concern grows as to if and when this growth will end.

In their concern to nip inflation in the bud, the Federal Reserve moved aggressively to negotiate a soft landing for the economy, to bring it down from a rate of growth which they think might be inflationary. And thus far, the strategy seems to have been working. The latest economic information we have showed that the economy in the second quarter was growing at an annual rate of something like 3.8 percent, for the first half of the year, an annual rate of 3.5 percent.

Now that's the full side of the story. What's the half-empty side of the story?

In the past, economic growth has always come with favorable outcomes with respect to two particular areas. One was job growth, and the second was income growth. That has been for a long time conventional economic wisdom: as long as the American economy was growing, one could count on a rising number of jobs, and the income position of individual wage earners would respond favorably to that rising growth.

Now, what has happened to cause us to reflect on that economic truism? Two things. First, in the United States this period of economic growth has not brought with it a dramatic increase in the total number of jobs.

Secondly, while indeed total income is rising as a consequence of this growth, the individual position of wage earners has not been growing with the rise in overall income. In effect, we have grown a number of jobs, but those jobs are not the same kinds of jobs that we saw growing in earlier periods, nor do they carry with them the same implications in terms of job security, wages and benefits. In effect, we have been lagging in terms of the quality of job growth. And one of the concomitants, particularly in the United States, has been an extraordinary growth in the inequality of income distribution in this country.

Not long ago, *Business Week* magazine, which by no means is regarded by anybody as a "left-wing, liberal rag," ran on its cover the following heading: "Inequality: How the growing gap between rich and poor in America is hurting the economy." What was striking about this is that *Business Week* clearly recognizes, as do a growing number of people, that the growing inequality itself threatens to change the very nature of the American economy, and the perception of fairness that has been attached to the American economy: Give people an opportunity to enter, and they can rise by their own wits and do well. That is no longer necessarily the case.

As the sense of fairness is being compromised, the growing gap between rich and poor in America is hurting the economy. That is a dramatic point of departure for economic theorists to consider, because as far as economic theory was concerned in the past, inequality in income growth was attributable to slow growth in the economy. What theorists are now beginning to understand is that inequality in income distribution may itself be a *contributor* to slow growth in the economy. The old economic notion that all that mattered was the aggregate amount of income is now being questioned.

What we have learned is that an increase in demands for goods and services across the industrialized world does not necessarily manifest itself as it did in the past, in an increase in the demand for workers. We are learning to do more with fewer people, and as a consequence of this enormous movement towards globalization and increased global competitiveness, we have opened up an extraordinary pool of labor resources that is now in competition around the world.

In 1980, the top 25 percent of income-earning families accounted for 48.2 percent of all income in the American economy. The bottom 25 percent accounted for 7.6 percent. By 1992, the top 25 percent's share had gone up to 51.3 percent. That was an increase of roughly $16,000, and it averaged out, in terms of average family income, to something in excess of $91,000 for the average family in the top 25 percent. The bottom 25 percent slipped from 7.6 percent of all income to 6.5 percent, producing an average family income of $11,530. That is below the poverty line for the average family of four as defined by the U.S. Department of Census. So what we have seen is an extraordinary widening of the gap in income distribution.

This is important for two reasons. First, because it does something to our perception of the fairness of the economic system. It says that even though we may pride ourselves or delude ourselves into thinking that everybody has equal access to opportunity to be a player in this economic game—which is in itself not true—the outcome seems to be less and less fair to those at the low end, whom I suspect work at least as hard, if not harder, than those in the top 25 percent. What Kevin Phillips, a Republican political strategist, and again, no bleeding heart liberal, says on this is, this growing income inequality "starts to make us into a different country."

I don't believe that this nation, given all of the social tensions that exist today, can hold together in the face of this kind of growing inequality in income. For those at the top who may perceive that they are advantaged by this process, what they are going to find is that more and more, that increased increment of income which they get is going to be spent on security systems, and walling themselves off into golden ghettos to isolate themselves from that growing segment of America that has no opportunity, or any likelihood of enhancing their well-being.

Secondly, and economists are finally becoming concerned about it, is that how that pie is sliced does have important implications for economic growth. In metropolitan areas with the widest differentials in income between the top and the bottom, the rates of economic growth and job creation has lagged behind those areas in which those income differentials were narrower. To the extent that the poor have no resources or minimal resources, they are not major contributors to economic growth. And it is that economic growth that has bumped up people at the high end of the income spectrum.

Why has this growing stratification occurred? There are a number of reasons. One is the diminishing power of labor unions in the United States. Labor unions in the United States at their high probably accounted for upwards of 25 percent of the total labor force. They are probably now down to about 11 percent. The decline in the demand for low-skilled labor in the United States has left out a vehicle for advancement for many people in the labor force. The dramatic increase in imports; the ready accessibility of American markets to overseas products; all of these things have been cited as reasons why the American economy has not been generating the kind of narrowing of income gaps that has occurred in other countries.

In Europe they have a different case. The income gap between the top and the bottom is much narrower than in the U.S., for a variety of reasons. One, they have very strong labor unions. Secondly, they have much higher minimum wages. Thirdly, there tends to be nationwide bargaining as opposed to industrial or plant-wide bargaining, as in the case of the United States. In Europe, income inequality is not the problem that it is in the United States. And if the Europeans want to pat themselves on the back, they have a right to. But, what has been the consequence of a social safety net, a legislative paradigm that concerns itself with narrow income differentials, in terms of job growth? They have not generated jobs. European economies have been essentially stagnant in terms of job creation. So the price that they have paid for trying to narrow the wage differential is minimal growth in employment, which means that their problems will take on a different coloration. Their problems will involve a growing burden on those who continue to work in order to sustain that social safety net that keeps the income gap from growing. And what we have seen as a consequence of that has been a growing restlessness on the part of a number of industrialized countries in Western Europe in particular, to high rates of taxation, high minimum wages, strong union activity and the like. In short, they too have problems. Their cup is equally as half empty as is ours.

What is happening, and you see it described in terms of rightsizing, downsizing, re-engineering the corporation, is a relentless pursuit of the minimalization of costs of production. Producers are now free to seek resources all over the world, and the only consideration is, what do I have to pay these resources to get the job done?

What we are seeing is a phenomenon called factor-price equalization. As competition increases from the local area to a wider area to encompass the globe, that factors of production are going to find that the return for their services in America is going to have to adjust to compensate for changes in the return for services for workers who do the same sort of thing in Sri Lanka.

That means that this growing wage inequality is going to change. The top is going to come down, the bottom is going to come up. But that change is going to bring with it enormous stresses and strains in industrialized economies. And it is not simply a case of suggesting that if we work smarter, we'll be better off than others, because the ability to get smarter is no longer impeded by access to knowledge. Communications is one of the fastest growing areas, and the ability to transfer knowledge and technology across national borders is astounding. We don't have any unique edge any longer in brain power, and as a college professor, I can assure you that what I see in the classroom doesn't auger very well for America's competitive prowess in the future.

It is against this backdrop of an economy that seems to be performing on its face reasonably well, but not generating as many goodies as it used to, that all of the social tensions have to be debated: issues of gender discrimination, or racial discrimination; issues of health care reform; issues of plant closures. All of these things are taking place against a backdrop of an economy that can no longer produce what we took for granted.

If all of us live long enough, the hope is that we will see a world profoundly transformed, where those at the very bottom may find that they have risen as a consequence of this global dynamic, while those at the top are going to be asked to make certain sacrifices. That's the ultimate dream. The question is, will such a dream ever be manifest? Will those who *have* willingly give that which they possess to accommodate this adjustment process that's inexorable? And the concern that I have is that they will not.

I will be candid and perhaps for an economist humble in saying to you, that the answer to these problems is probably not going to come from economics. That what ultimately we have to be concerned with is economic justice. If we care about the world that our children and grandchildren are going to live in, then we had better give a damn about economic justice. And all the tweaking by economists isn't going to necessarily provide us with any clear answers to these problems, because in the final analysis, where the answer lies is in each of us.

You see, Walt Kelly was absolutely right when he wrote in his strip, *Pogo,* "we have met the enemy and he is us." Unless and until there is an extraordinary transformation in the hearts and minds of each of us as human beings, until and unless we are willing to acknowledge our responsibility for our neighbors in community, there will never be the appropriate kind of background against which positive legislation can go forward.

Legislators do not lead, they only follow. And until the social economic paradigm is changed and the message become unequivocally clear to our legislators, that we understand that this situation cannot be allowed to persist, that we must accept responsibility, and the legislation to structure those responsibilities on a national and international level must be forthcoming, nothing's going to happen.

Section Three:

Tales of Values
Reflections on Meaning and Purpose

A Tale of Values
OCTOBER, 2007

This above all: to thine own self be true,
And it must follow, as the night the day,
Thou canst not then be false to any man.

—FROM ACT 1, SCENE III OF HAMLET, BY WILLIAM SHAKESPEARE

For some time now, National Public Radio (NPR) has had a morning feature called "Story Corps: Recording America." The premise is quite simple: to interview ordinary people and to record in their own words whatever story that individual chose to share. And, though the stories might not be the stuff that makes headlines, they offer interesting and personal insights into the lives of people with whom we might unknowingly interact on any given day.

On this particular morning, I heard a simple but compelling personal story about a gentleman who for the past 45 years has served as a doorman at the Plaza Hotel in New York City. Having grown up in New York City myself, perhaps it was his unmistakable New York City accent that drew me to his story. His name is Ed Trinka, and he took this job on his graduation from high school. It was his very first job. To many, being a doorman, even at a hotel as world-renowned as the Plaza, might seem rather mundane. Yet, for Ed Trinka, he sees himself as an ambassador of sorts, offering a friendly "Good morning" and a smile to passers-by. His own words provide a window into his personal philosophy: "That's what it's all about, being in front there and smiling and just making everybody happy. That's the whole thing of it." He adds, "You know, anybody that comes in there is a VIP. And when they tell me, 'Treat them like a VIP,' I say I already do." But, what was so profoundly moving for me was his revelation of a piece of advice that his father had shared with him. "You know, my father told me years ago… 'Be such a man and live such a life that if everybody lived a life like yours, this would be God's paradise.' And, I go by that."

His words triggered in me a recollection of another man, whom I had known, whose own life had been a testament to his humility, hard work, and integrity in his dealings with others. A family man with four children, he too had been a New Yorker. When the Great Depression struck, he was fortunate enough to have a job as a cab driver, working the night shift for 17 years, with no complaints, grateful that he had a source of support for his family. At the age of 46, he lost his wife to cancer. Still, with the help of an aged relative who spoke not a word of English, he kept the family together, overseeing the marriage of two of his daughters and then moving to Los Angeles for a new start with his two remaining children. He purchased a small grocery store, and took on a partner, a relative who had considerable experience in the grocery business, an act of generosity that was to have sad consequences. Along the way, his remaining daughter married and, 5 years after he was widowed, he was fortunate to find and to wed a new life partner who would work by his side and provide both him and his son with a loving home.

His initial partner turned out to be a compulsive gambler, who stole proceeds from the small business, leaving him with a mountain of debt. Facing a threat of bankruptcy, he called a meeting of his creditors and offered them an alternative to a return of pennies on the dollar. If they would work with him and give him time, he promised them 100 cents on the dollar. They accepted his offer, and after more than a year of hard work and sacrifice, the old debts were repaid in full.

In time, he would purchase a larger neighborhood grocery store that he and his wife would run until his retirement. Scrupulous in his dealings with his customers, the business was successful. To those customers who requested a credit account, he offered it to them, at no interest charge. The trust that he engendered was repaid many times over by customers who, in settling their accounts at months-end, would present him with a signed blank check telling him to fill in the amount that was owed. Like the Plaza doorman, he too would greet people with a ready smile. Throughout his life, he was grateful for whatever material gains he had made, but always with the attitude that his life had been good, and whatever circumstance he enjoyed it was always "the best." In smoggy Los Angeles, if you were to comment to him about the smog, his response would be, "…It may be smoggy elsewhere, but there is no smog on my block." And, he was sincere in his belief. He enjoyed his retirement for more than two decades, and took pleasure in seeing his son marry and add two more grandchildren to the family. And, when he passed away in his late eighties, though he was unable to speak, I suspect that he would have offered no complaints for the lot he had drawn in life.

He was at best a quite ordinary man, much like the Plaza Hotel doorman, with a pleasant demeanor, humble, hard-working, and honest beyond reproach. His worldly possessions were modest, but he left a legacy, especially to his only son, which was priceless and rich beyond any material measure. I am that son; he was my father, my "old man." I think of him often, and hope that his son has proven to be the man he would have wished. From time to time, I find myself reflecting upon a particular quote that was attributed to Albert Einstein. It has been on my desk for many years and is a favorite of mine. Perhaps it was the memory of my father that had directed me to it. It reads, *"Try not to become a man of success, but rather a man of value.*" What good fortune has been mine to have had as my role model such a "man of value" as my "old man."

Of Old Friends and the Kindness of a Stranger
NOVEMBER, 2008

Remember there's no such thing as a small act of kindness.
Every act creates a ripple with no logical end.
—SCOTT ADAMS

Love and kindness are never wasted. They always make a difference.
They bless the one who receives them, and they bless you, the giver.
—BARBARA DE ANGELIS

You cannot do a kindness too soon, for you never know how soon it will be too late.
—RALPH WALDO EMERSON

I must confess that I do not have the option of "caller ID" on my home phone. Thus, when either my wife or I have an incoming phone call, we have no idea whether the caller is familiar to us or not until we engage the voice at the other end of the line. And, we certainly do welcome calls from our many friends. At the same time, the sheer number of telephone solicitations associated with the recent election campaign aroused in me an almost intuitive and rather surly response when the phone rang and the caller was not familiar either to me or to my wife. Quite recently, I was distracted by an incoming call. Initially, I could not recognize the caller's voice and my own tone was, therefore, rather clipped. Still, the voice at the other end of the line offered me anecdotal evidence that indicated that we were not strangers. Finally, after I confessed my embarrassment at my inability to recognize him straightaway, it suddenly dawned on me that this was the voice of an old and good friend with whom I had not spoken for more than twenty years.

He and I had been colleagues and friends more than forty years ago, when we both were working as economists in the research department of the Federal Reserve Bank of Philadelphia. Sometime in 1969 or thereabouts, we had gone our separate ways. Other than a brief visit with him in the interim, we had not spoken with each other for lo those many years. His call had prompted many reminiscences about the many pleasant occasions we had enjoyed, as well as some catching up on what had transpired in our lives since last we had met. Our conversation also served to rekindle our recollection of a chance meeting with a perfect stranger at an airport and an act of kindness from him that would have a profound impact on our lives.

Both he and I had registered to attend a professional meeting of economists that was to be held in Chicago in December 1968. Thus, we found ourselves in a jetliner en route from Philadelphia to Chicago. The flight had proceeded without incident until the plane was approaching the environs of Chicago. At this point the Captain came on the intercom to announce that a lake-effect snowstorm had created blizzard-like conditions throughout the Chicago area, and that all incoming and outgoing flight operations had been suspended at O'Hare airport until further notice. He further informed us that our flight would be placed in a holding pattern, orbiting O'Hare on the chance that a break in the weather might allow us to land. After more than an hour or so of circling over Chicago, our pilot told us that we would overfly Chicago and proceed north to Milwaukee, the closest open airport that could accommodate our aircraft. Once on the ground, we could board the waiting ground transportation that had been arranged to take us to Chicago. Our baggage was not among the earliest batch that had been taken from the plane. By the time we reclaimed it, we learned that there were not enough buses to accommodate all the passengers, and those that had been available had already left for Chicago with as many passengers as they could hold. Regrettably, we would have to wait until additional ground transport could be arranged.

While we were waiting, I approached the ticket counter of one of the regional carriers that served Chicago to inquire as to if and/or when flight operations from Milwaukee to Chicago might resume. I was told the weather was expected to break within an hour or two, and their flight from Milwaukee to Chicago had seats available. We agreed that this was desirable. As best as my friend and I can recall after nearly forty years, we had not yet been issued the tickets when we were approached by a gentleman who explained that he had heard me asking about a possible flight to Chicago. It was a chance meeting that would have consequences that my friend and I have pondered to this very day, though at the time we had no way of knowing it.

He explained to us that he lived midway between Milwaukee and Chicago. He had been planning to drive home from Milwaukee and had hired and paid for a rental car at the airport for that purpose. If we agreed to drive him to his home, my friend and I would be welcome to take the car the rest of the way to our hotel in Chicago where we could drop it off at no expense to us. Faced with an indeterminate wait for a bus to take us to Chicago, or a flight that might not take off for another hour or more, we accepted his offer. As a gesture of thanks, I volunteered to drive. We loaded our bags into the rental car and I started driving south from the airport. The weather was still ugly and the snow and sleet made the driving treacherous. As I drove through the storm, I reflected more than once as to whether our acceptance of our passenger's offer had been the right choice. Finally, he instructed me to pull off the interstate and directed me to his home. He thanked us for getting him safely home, and I resumed the drive to Chicago. My friend and I were both grateful to arrive at our hotel in one piece, and I dropped the car off as I had been instructed to do. We checked into our rooms, and I was certainly ready to put that strange encounter and the harrowing drive that ensued behind us.

When I got to my room, I put my bag on the bed and, perhaps from force of habit, I turned on the TV. The image and the text seemed to leap out from the screen. An incoming airliner from Milwaukee had crashed upon landing at O'Hare airport and among the fifty or so passengers on the plane, more than half had been killed. It was the very flight we had been poised to take, had it not been for the intercession of a perfect stranger and his kind offer. I immediately called my friend to inform him of what had occurred, and it was only then that we both realized that, there but for an act of grace, our lives might well have ended.

In the years since that occurrence, I have continued to ponder that chance meeting with a stranger whose act of kindness might literally have saved both my life and that of my friend. Why did he choose to engage me rather than someone else? I recalled that he was carrying a small black suitcase identical to my own. He had noted that fact when he spoke to me. My wife had just purchased the bag for me since I had lacked a case of that size. Could my wife's decision to make that purchase have served to trigger a series of events that would result in that chance meeting and its attendant consequences? And, there was something else about the mysterious Samaritan that remains etched into my consciousness, and that adds a further, almost mystical element to that event so many years removed. The name of that perfect stranger was Edward Beau Geste. In French, Beau Geste translates into "gallant (or "gracious) gesture." Was this just another coincidence in what for me remains an inexplicable example of chance events precipitated by an act of kindness?

Whatever were the circumstances that caused our paths to cross that snowy night so long ago, I shall never be able to forget that act of kindness, that "gallant gesture" from a perfect stranger that has made such a difference in my life. I would certainly hope that my own experience has sensitized me to the notion that I should not squander an opportunity to offer my own kindness to others. Perhaps that is what Margaret Cho had in mind when she offered the words, "Sometimes when we are generous in small, barely detectable ways it can change someone's life forever." Amen to that!!

What's In a Word?
FEBRUARY, 2008

Well before the first Tuesday in November, we will have been exposed to a seemingly unending stream of political advertisements, or "sound bites," that may assault our sensibilities and/or insult our intelligence. And, as has so often been the case in recent years, one descriptor is sure to be used again and again as a pejorative designed to label the candidate against whom it is directed, and serve as an indictment of their character and a sign of their unworthiness to be considered for public office.

The word to which I refer is "liberal."

What is there about the word that, for so many, has become inflammatory and reviled? What does it mean to be a liberal? Is liberalism truly an evil from which this republic must be delivered, as is posited by right-wing media personality and author Sean Hannity in his latest tract, or by the blather of such ideologues as Rush Limbaugh or Ann Coulter? Or, has the word come to be redefined by right-wing spin masters and used as a club relentlessly to disparage and batter anyone who might not subscribe to their vision for America and the world?

Regrettably, we live in a time when far too few of us have a sense of our historical roots, and of the struggles that had to be fought and won so that we might take for granted many of the benefits we enjoy today as workers and as citizens of this nation. In addition, many of us seem to have surrendered our capacity for critical thinking. Thus, what passes for political enlightenment is a series of 15- or 30-second ads that portray the opposition candidate in a very unfavorable light. In addition, increasingly since the initiation of our "war against terrorism," anyone tainted with the label of being a liberal is also somehow falsely assumed to be lacking in patriotism. But, my brief is not to examine the malevolence of those who rail against liberals by gratuitously wrapping themselves in the flag. Rather, it is to remind readers of the extraordinary legacy of which we are beneficiaries as a result of the initiatives of liberals or progressive thinkers.

Just a partial list constitutes a remarkable testimonial to the efforts of our liberal and more progressive forebears. In the workplace, the abolition of child labor, the eight-hour workday, the minimum wage, unemployment benefits and disability insurance are just a sampling of what liberals have fought for and achieved. Even as many on the political right were professing their support for families and for family values, it took ongoing pressure from liberals to pass the Family Leave Act, allowing workers to take a period of unpaid leave to attend to family members who required attention. If the air we breathe and the water we drink are freer of pollutants, give thanks to liberals for having championed legislation that gave us the Environmental Protection Agency (EPA). If our workplaces are safer, then we can look to the Occupational Safety and Health Administration (OSHA) for having made employers make them so. Social Security and Medicare/Medicaid have helped to make retirement a little more secure, and have reduced some of the angst over access to healthcare that comes with advancing years and/or inadequate means to afford such care. Although men have long enjoyed the right to vote, it took ongoing struggle by and with people of liberal persuasion to give women the same right to that franchise. The struggle for civil rights is another cause which had liberals in the forefront. Thanks to the Securities and Exchange Commission (SEC), we have greater transparency as regards information that allows investors to make more informed decisions. Deposit insurance from the Federal Deposit Insurance Corporation (FDIC) and the Federal Savings and Loan Insurance Corporation (FSLIC) affords people greater security that their deposits are safe, as well as regulatory oversight of financial institutions. The Food and Drug Administration (FDA) provides us with necessary regulatory oversight that helps to make the food we eat and the medicines we take safer. And, on and on the list could go.

However, in each of the above examples, entrenched opposition had to be overcome in order to make them manifest. That many now take the fruits of these measures for granted should not make us forget what it took to put them in place.

I firmly believe that each of us must accept our individual responsibility in shaping our lives and the outcomes we seek. At the same time, I continue to believe that there remains an important and ongoing role for government, in concert with our own efforts as individuals, to make this nation more fully live up to its promise to *all* of us as citizens. And, I readily acknowledge, along with others of more conservative political leaning, the legitimacy of the ongoing deliberation over the appropriate role and size of government to best serve the citizens of this nation. We should all be mindful of the danger of excessive power, public *or* private. For, as was opined by Thomas Jefferson, "Eternal vigilance is the price of liberty." At the same time, I would not identify with the overly simplistic assessment of the late former President Ronald Reagan that, "Government is not the solution to our problems; it is the problem." Rather, I would say by way of rebuttal, "It is bad government that is the problem. Surely, the wave of corporate malfeasance and greed exemplified by the scandalous behavior of Enron and others furnishes a compelling example of the harm perpetrated upon our society by the excesses of unrestrained private power. However, I would hope that the discourse over the appropriate limits of power can be conducted without impugning the character of the discussants. In that spirit, while I share with my more conservative counterparts the desire that our government should spend our tax dollars and conduct the public's business wisely, I also accept the notion that the taxes I pay represent the price that must be paid for a civil society.

It is altogether regrettable that, in their zeal to demonize all liberal thought, the more zealous proponents of this view have polarized this nation and chosen to assail the character and the patriotism of those who do not share their views. Thus, while I value the friendship of many individuals of a more conservative disposition, and remain more than willing to engage in a civil discussion of our philosophical differences, I will readily and unashamedly acknowledge that I am a "liberal," and I take pride in the extraordinarily rich legacy to which I am heir.

On Discerning Between Dissent and Disloyalty

JANUARY, 2006

Webster's Dictionary defines "dissent" as, "to differ in opinion; to disagree." The word "disloyalty," on the other hand, is defined as, "lack of loyalty; a violation of allegiance." Within a pluralistic political arena, there has been a long and well established practice of operating within an environment in which dissent or disagreement is not only tolerated, but is seen as a sign of a healthy body politic. Thus, frequently those who may find themselves disagreeing with their fellow legislators are referred to as "the loyal opposition," a characterization that clearly recognizes that one may dissent without being disloyal. Indeed, the hallmark of a democratic society is its innate recognition of the right of its citizens to express their disagreement or dissent without fear of recrimination or allegations of disloyalty.

However, even democratic societies may, from time to time in periods of perceived national emergency, find themselves equating dissent with disloyalty. Each such occasion should serve to remind us that the nation is poorly served when our fundamental right to voice our disagreement or displeasure is compromised through intimidation and/or charges that expressing criticism of public policy is tantamount to being an enemy of the state. Lest there be any doubt that dissent directed towards even a most powerful and popular leader is a necessary ingredient to sustain a democratic society, one should reflect on the words of Theodore Roosevelt uttered in 1918, at a time when this nation was at war: "To announce that there must be no criticism of the president, or that we are to stand by the president, right or wrong, is not only unpatriotic and servile, but is morally treasonable to the American public." In other words, leadership carries with it an obligation to respect and to tolerate contrary opinions.

To be sure, business organizations do not necessarily operate in the same manner as do political institutions; they may not be wholly democratic procedurally. Neither do successful business organizations operate in an entirely autocratic fashion. For, the essence of autocracy is that it is governed or led by someone who has independent or self-derived power that imparts a sense of absolute right. Autocratic leaders, therefore, lead without feeling any need to have or to reflect upon contrary opinions. One may ask, are the best interests of the organization well served by a leader with an oversized ego, who not only fails to invite dissent, but who may impugn the loyalty of anyone with the courage to offer a contrary opinion? Or, is a leader so lacking in self-confidence that (s)he may regard any dissent as a personal affront or challenge to his/her authority? Can an organization, so led, thrive in an environment of accelerating change and competitive pressures, where leaders need to be open to alternative or disparate views or ideas with regard to those critical issues with which the enterprise must contend if it is to be successful?

In his seminal work on leadership, "Leadership Is An Art," Max DePree, then Chairman of the Board of Herman Miller, Inc., offers a number of pithy observations regarding the essence of leadership. An effective leader must have self-confidence and clear thinking, particularly with regard to his/her own beliefs. For, absent a clear sense of *what* one believes and *why,* such a leader could not possess the self-confidence to expose those beliefs to the challenge of dissent. Such a sense of confidence is contagious and serves to "rally the troops" in the pursuit of the goals towards which the organization is striving. At the same time, such self-confidence should not devolve into a sense of infallibility, for such hubris does not countenance dissent. But, with the confidence that can only come from continually testing one's own ideas against those of others, DePree asserts that leaders will "encourage contrary opinions" and "abandon themselves to the strength of others." In reality, then, a true leader must be a *listener,* open to the ideas of others, not as a threat to his/her own beliefs, but as a means of validating those beliefs.

Of all the assets that any business or organization may have at its disposal, arguably the most valuable of them is its people. The collective experience, wisdom and insights regarding the enterprise and its operating environment that is embedded in these people constitute an invaluable reservoir of ideas from which the leader may fill her/his cup. However, the willingness to do so will vary directly with the degree to which the leader possesses the strength of character and confidence, without suspicion, freely to invite the opinions of others. On the other hand, in an organization where the leader cannot discern the difference between honest dissent and disloyalty, that reservoir is unlikely to be filled, nor will it be tapped.

Although the democratic paradigm might not apply in full to a business or professional organization, the virtues of dissent are nonetheless applicable. And, the observation of the late Senator J. William Fulbright with regard to value of dissent is still surely worth noting. He observed that, "In a democracy, dissent is an act of faith. Like medicine, the test of its value is not in its taste, but its effects." Therefore, the tonic of dissent within an organization should not be dismissed out of hand as an expression of disloyalty. Rather, it may reflect the strongest remedy, which, if ministered on a regular basis, may assure the continued good health of its recipient. For, as the late English historian and mathematician Jacob Bronowski opined, "Has there ever been a society that died of dissent? Several have died of conformity in our lifetime."

Embracing Change
SEPTEMBER, 2004

It has been said of the many things that we confront in life, two things are inevitable, death and taxes. On reflection, however, surely we should add at least one more entry to that rather short list, namely *change*. For, is it not amply clear that change is a constant presence that affects us whether we like it or not? We must contend with it, or risk being reduced to irrelevancy. But if change is a constant in our lives, the manner in which we choose to respond to it can make all the difference in its impact upon us.

The essence of all change is that it is disruptive; it makes different that which it acts upon. What has been familiar and unquestioned by us has been transformed in some way, and is now less familiar or less comfortable for us to deal with. It is human nature to take comfort in the familiar. Once we have settled into a routine, we have a tendency to eschew that which is disruptive and unknown in its impact. For that reason, more often than not, when confronted with the prospect of change, we may choose to dig in our heels and resist. In other words, when dealing with change, rather than being *proactive* and welcoming or embracing it, we are more often *reactive* and reluctant to act.

In the physical universe, we are presented with ample evidence of the ongoing process of change and its consequences, both positive and negative. Nature demonstrates to us with regularity that the key to survival lies in the capacity to accommodate or adjust to change. Where species have adapted to change successfully, they have evolved and preserved their continuity. In the increasingly competitive environment of business, it is certainly no less true that the failure to anticipate the forces of change and/or to adapt to them may threaten the ongoing survival of the enterprise. For, as the global marketplace has expanded the range of opportunities for business organizations, it has simultaneously meted out harsh penalties to those organizations that have failed adequately to embrace and accommodate the change dynamic.

There is, I believe, a lesson in the above for each of us as individuals. The process of successful and rewarding growth, whether corporate or individual, or intellectual, professional, or personal growth, entails the same kind of adaptation to change that is required in the natural world to assure the continuity of the species. Yet there is within each of us a reluctance to abandon the known, the routine, for the path of uncertainty that is a concomitant of change. But, if life is to be an adventure rather than following the same routine day in and day out, perhaps we should pay heed to the words of the poet Robert Frost. In his poem, "The Road Not taken," he writes:

"Two roads diverged in a wood, and I—
I took the one less traveled by,
And that has made all the difference."

Or, if we should choose to seek wisdom regarding change from "the mouths of babes," then we might reflect upon the words of young Calvin, the mischievous principal character of a comic strip. "Calvin and Hobbes," that is no longer published. In speaking to his fictional playmate and companion Hobbes, his stuffed tiger, Calvin observes:

> "Change is invigorating! If you don't accept new challenges, you become complacent and lazy! Your life atrophies! New experiences lead to new questions and new solutions! Change forces us to experiment and adapt! That's how we learn and grow."

If I may offer a parting word of advice to the readers of this essay, it is simply that you too might consider "taking the path less traveled," by reaching out and welcoming the opportunity for further growth that comes from embracing change.

Managers and Leaders: They're Not the Same

MARCH, 2005

A recent issue of *Business Week* magazine carried an editorial commentary noting the problems that Lawrence Summers, President of Harvard University, had encountered in trying to accomplish an ambitious agenda. His leadership style apparently had impacted adversely on his ability to move Harvard in the strategic direction he sought. Whether or not this setback is only transitory remains to be seen. However, it does serve to point out the difficulties that are inherent in the leadership position within organizations. That same article also made mention of several other high profile executives in observing that, "Summers joins the ranks of recent leaders brought in to generate change in organizations only to misfire and fail." Among them were Durk Jager at Procter and Gamble, Howell Raines at *The New York Times,* and Carly Fiorina at Hewlett-Packard. Whatever may have been their strategic intent, *Business Week* notes, "Good intentions are no substitute for good management."

Surely, one of the conditions that must apply for any business, whether large or small or in-between, is that it has to be skillfully managed. And, while such an observation might not strike the reader as terribly insightful, it is equally the case that, while good management may raise the odds of success, even a well managed business has no guarantee of success. This is all the more true in an environment within which the winds of change are both omnipotent and accelerating. Because all change is disruptive by nature, it imposes a special challenge for those charged with management responsibilities. At the same time, when change is anticipated well in advance, there is a far greater likelihood that management can more successfully manage it to the advantage of the organization, or, at the very least, minimize any adverse impacts that may befall an enterprise when it is hit with "surprising" changes in its market environment.

Globalization has greatly speeded-up the forces of change and, correspondingly, has enhanced the need to skillfully anticipate and manage change. In that regard, workers should be sensitive to a changing environment and take it upon themselves to inform their manager of any new information which might be useful in directional decision-making. Even so, as noted above, good management alone is no guarantor of success. For, while good management may be *necessary* to assure success and profitability, it is not *sufficient* if there is an absence of strong and purposeful leadership with the organization.

Inside any organization, if people do not carry out their function as producers, the work will not get done. However, no matter how highly skilled and motivated the workers or producers may be, in the absence of an established and workable structure or system of procedures, it would be difficult, if not impossible, to avoid role conflicts and a lack of clarity in responsibilities among the producers/employees. Thus, the key responsibility of *managers* is to make sure that the necessary structures and/or systems, as well as the needed resources, are in place and are being utilized properly so the work can get done efficiently.

Nonetheless, just as desire without effort is unlikely to generate results, good workers who are well-managed may be of little avail if the organization is poorly led. For, the essential role of the *leader* is to provide the strategic vision or direction that makes clear where the organization should be going, and to fashion an operational plan robust enough to allow the enterprise to successfully deal with those changes it may confront. In doing so, he/she must take the point in constantly monitoring the market environment and in anticipating the nature of those changes that may lie ahead and offer positive opportunities, as well as pose problems or threats to ongoing success. Absent that strategic vision, the enterprise is like a ship without a rudder or a helmsman, tossed about by the ever-shifting winds of change and competition with little chance of successfully reaching a safe harbor. A survey of the landscape of industry here and abroad would show that it is replete with the wreckage of proud businesses that faltered, but not necessarily for want of good workers or competent managers. Rather, as noted earlier, the leaders' vision was flawed, and he/she failed either to anticipate the winds of change transforming his/her market environment, or to design a plan that would allow the organization successfully to tack in the face of those winds.

In many such cases, when leadership fails and the organization is adrift without strategic direction, its primary focus becomes fixed on becoming more *efficient,* or, on "doing things right," rather than on being more *effective,* or, on "doing the right things." Old rules, systems and procedures that may have worked well in the past become more rigid and codified, even as they become less relevant and more hurtful to the organization. And, for want of attention to *the top line,* which speaks to where the organization should be headed, invariably *the bottom line* suffers, or worse, the business fails. Thus, competent and visionary leaders in businesses of all sizes set the tone for success. Before one can manage a successful business, it must first and foremost be pointed in that direction that will most assure it a fighting chance to attain that success. That is the pivotal role of the leader.

On Standing Out in a Crowd
MAY, 2005

There is an old saw that goes, "Where does an 800-pound gorilla sit?" And, the answer is, as most of us know, "anywhere he wants to." The message is, "If you are big enough, you can do pretty much as you please." It seems as though that message is furnishing the script for much of what is going on in today's intensely competitive business climate. Reflective of today's "800-pound gorillas," the extraordinary ascendancy of Wal-Mart, the retailing colossus, and the growth and success of other "big box, category killers" such as Home Depot, as well as such franchisors as Starbucks, among others, has cast a giant shadow across the competitive marketplace. In such an environment, the owners of many of today's small-to-medium-sized business firms may be excused for pondering whether in the future there will still be a place for them at the table.

To be sure, size alone is no guarantor of success, and a huge number of America's small and medium-sized firms are alive and well, and are likely to remain so in the foreseeable future. That is the good news. However, this good news must be tempered with the realization that, for any business owner, success is a fragile thing that cannot be taken for granted. As always, its attainment and sustainability involves an ongoing struggle that requires perseverance and dedication. And, given the drive towards bigness in the marketplace, smaller business owners must focus on those things that will help to make them stand out in a crowd, lest they run the risk of disappearing in the shadow of their taller competitors. In the face of an increasingly successful, if impersonal medium of trade and commerce, the Internet, perhaps one surprising lesson that is emerging for businessmen and women is the value of the "personal" touch in achieving sales success. Thus, a paradox in this age of electronic commerce is that, to stand out from a crowded field of competitors, one tool that may serve you exceedingly well is the "low-tech," but time-tested approach of personal selling as a means of keeping your customers and growing your business.

There is a sizable body of research that confirms that far more time and effort is required to attract a *new* customer than to retain an *existing* one. Thus, the arithmetic is persuasive that any business would be well-served if it could be more successful in retaining its customer base. This does not mean that one should ignore the virtue of growing that base in order to stay ahead of the inevitable attrition and loss of customers that may be expected to occur over time in spite of one's best efforts to minimize such losses. In any case, the ability to interject the personal dimension into the sales process may provide you with an advantage that would be hard to replicate via the electronic sales medium. Needless to say, without a quality offering at a fair price, no amount of personal involvement is likely to spawn much success. At the same time, it should be recognized that the advantage that size affords through economies of scale, when it comes to the pricing of a product or service, makes trying to compete on price alone a losing proposition for most, if not all, smaller businesses. Thus, in today's increasingly competitive market setting, where both low prices *and* high quality are prerequisites for making a sale, the advantage of a more personalized sales regimen should be all the more apparent as an integral part of gaining a winning edge.

How then to stand out in a crowd? It may seem overly simplistic to assert that, if you want to stand out in a crowd, your customers must recognize you. To survive and to thrive amidst "800-pound gorillas" requires that small/medium-sized business owners must be regarded as much more than simply "another vendor" by their customers. That means that you must be much more than a series of keystrokes on a computer screen, within only a single stroke of the "Delete" key from having your sales initiative dispatched to the electronic trashcan. When you communicate with your customers, they must readily associate both your face and your voice with your company name. No amount of E-mail can substitute for those attributes in establishing a personal/professional relationship with your customers. Since that will require a greater expenditure of your time, it is imperative that you clearly identify those customers whose business potential is worthy of your added investment in time. Remember, *not all customers are equal.* Once you have identified your most valued existing customers and potential additions, you must work to build those relationships on the basis of integrity, mutual trust, and value. Your customers must come to see you not simply as a reliable supplier, but also as a confidant, someone with whom they are comfortable and who can help them in solving their problems. Above all, before you offer *your* words, be sure to cultivate one of Stephen R. Covey's "Seven Habits of Highly Effective People:" "Seek first to understand, then to be understood." That means that you must become a skilled and active listener in order to truly understand the needs and concerns of the other party. As you listen, build on what you hear to ask insightful, probing questions that can be of help in understanding how you might best serve his/her needs. That will require that you become more knowledgeable not only about your own business, but that of your customer(s) as well.

    The practical end sought in becoming more personally involved with your customers is to make clear that your interest goes beyond simply making *this* sale. Rather, you are seeking to build a long-term relationship, one in which you will be recognized as much more than simply a salesperson. If you can establish your credibility as a problem-solver, whose skill and experience are integral parts of a total value package that you can offer to your customers, you will have made *their* success, in part, dependent upon *your own*. In turn, that will give them a vested interest in your success that will help to establish a mutually supportive relationship, one far more likely to thrive in a sea of faceless and impersonal competitors whose only advantage derives in offering a lower price. In the increasingly impersonal world of commerce, might it not be a significant tactical and strategic oversight to surrender to your competitors the one tool that can truly serve to distinguish you from them? Thus, a key to standing out in a crowd might well be to put your "person" into personal selling.

Make Your Light Shine
DECEMBER, 2007

Make the most of yourself, for that is all there is of you.
—RALPH WALDO EMERSON

What lies behind us and what lies before us are tiny matters compared to what lies within us.
—RALPH WALDO EMERSON

I am quite sure that for many readers of this essay, there have been occasions when they have chosen to dine in a restaurant that offered Chinese cuisine. For those who have had one or more such experiences, irrespective of the gustatory quality of the offerings, there was at least one aspect to that experience that was a constant. After the server deposited the bill for the meal on your table, he/she would offer the diners a fortune cookie. And, who among us would fail to break open the cookie in order to retrieve the text of the "fortune" that presumably might await us at some future turn?

My well-worn Webster's New Collegiate Dictionary defines the term "fortune" as "That which falls to one; good or ill success or luck; esp., favorable issue." In that regard, any fortune that I may have been fated to receive has thus far eluded me. Indeed, more often than not, rather than containing notification of a possible fortune in my future, the cookie contained such aphorisms as, *Haste makes waste,* or *He who laughs last laughs loudest,* or some other piece of advice or maxim that we have heard on countless previous occasions. In short, the fortune cookie experience is for most of us basically ritualistic, offering us an opportunity light-heartedly to compare "fortunes" with others at our table, without giving the matter any serious further thought. For my youngest daughter and me, the fortune cookie experience has been an ongoing source of amusement for some time ever since she inquired of me what message my cookie contained, and I replied, *Help!! I am a prisoner in a Chinese fortune cookie factory.*

However, I recently found myself surprised at the message that greeted me upon extracting it from a fortune cookie. For it read, *You stand in your own light. Make it Shine.* How often is it that we might receive an admonition so profound from such an unlikely source? Upon returning to my desk, I found myself pondering the message. And, as I thought about it, I became increasingly convinced that, insofar as I was concerned, I had some way to go before my luminescence would be readily visible from a distance. If that were indeed true in my case, might it not also be true for countless other individuals? And, as an economist, that realization suggested to me that we as a society might very well be suffering a significant loss in terms of the gap between our productive efforts and our inherent potential. For, how many of us can truly make the case that, in our lives, we are doing the very best we can?

We are, each of us, multidimensional individuals by nature, and each day we are called on to draw upon one or more of those dimensions that define us. Our response to those calls will chart the extent to which our actions reflect our full engagement or some level of effort far short of that which we might be capable of giving. In our chosen profession or vocation, we are more likely than not to be a part of a larger organization or team. In such a setting, our efforts will help to determine the overall outcome of the larger body as a whole. Thus, when our exertions fall short of what they could be; when we fail to draw fully on our inner strengths; both we and those who may depend upon us are burdened with the shortfall from our own sub-optimal performance. Rather than making our light and that of those around us shine more brightly, we do the opposite. We make dimmer that which might have been more brightly illumined by a more robust effort on our part. Is not this example, with regard to the workplace, not equally applicable to a variety of settings in which we have roles and responsibilities to discharge? In our family unit, do our homes resonate with a sense of caring and love for each other? Do our children and our spouse see in us someone worthy of their affection and emulation? Do we take care to strike a proper balance between time spent with family and time spent in search of further, marginally valued accumulation of material goods? How often do we find ourselves "buying" the affection of those we love with "stuff" to assuage our inner sense of guilt for having denied them the far more priceless gift of our time? And, can we not also make the case that as members of a larger community, its wellbeing ultimately depends upon our level of engagement and participation? In the final analysis, are we not the keepers of our sisters and brothers, and the stewards of this fragile planet that we have sullied both by acts of omission and commission on our part?

Charles Dickens observed, "All of us have wonders hidden in our breasts, only needing circumstances to evoke them." Perhaps our failure oft times to draw on our strength when circumstances call is a reflection of our self-doubt, or a sense of inadequacy that we are capable of rising to whatever circumstances might befall us. Yet, perhaps the ultimate paradox might be that it is not our weaknesses, but our strengths to which we give short shrift. Marianne Williamson, in her book, *A Return to Love: Reflections on the Principles of a Course in Miracles (1992),* addresses the above paradox observing:

> "Our deepest fear is not that we are inadequate. Our deepest fear is that we are powerful beyond measure. It is our light, not our darkness that most frightens us. We ask ourselves, Who am I to be brilliant, gorgeous, talented, fabulous? Actually, who are you not to be? You are a child of God. Your playing small does not serve the world. …We are all meant to shine, as children do. … And as we let our own light shine, we unconsciously give other people permission to do the same. As we are liberated from our own fear, our presence automatically liberates others."

Like a muscle of the body that atrophies from inactivity, our inner strengths will wane if we fail constantly to employ them to their fullest when we are called upon to do so for the greater good. Rather than "hiding your light under a bushel" in obeisance to a sense of modesty or misplaced humility, *make your light shine.* And, in so doing, light the path for others to do the same.

On Measuring Success
JANUARY, 2006

It would not be an understatement to say that we are a success-driven culture. And, for many, if not most, the principal measure of success that we employ is a material one, namely one's net worth. Thus, people such as Bill Gates and Warren Buffet are regarded as particularly successful by virtue of the wealth they have amassed, as well as for their generosity. In this regard, CNN recently reported on a study by TNS Financial Services, a market research and polling firm, which noted that the ranks of millionaire households have grown substantially in recent years. According to this study, "Households with a net worth of at least $1 million excluding primary residences rose 8 percent to a record high 8.9 million." The same study also reported that "the number of 'emerging affluent' households, defined as households with a net worth between $100,000 and $500,000, excluding primary residences, is also on the rise." These households now number 24.5 million, up from 23.9 million last year. In commenting on this development, the manager of the study made the point that "the millionaire households don't grow rich overnight; the growth is largely due to measured planning and active reinvestment." And, it seems safe to say that for America's newly-minted millionaires, as well as for those emerging aspirants, crossing that net worth threshold would be seen by them, and by countless non-millionaire observers, as a clear and unassailable symbol of success.

Paradoxically, one can readily find substantive evidence in our society that, in the face of increasing Gross Domestic Product (GDP) and increasing wealth for many, such material success has not necessarily translated into correspondingly greater personal happiness.

Undoubtedly, many readers are familiar with this philosophical offering: "Money doesn't necessarily make you happy. But, if I'm going to be unhappy, I'd rather be unhappy *with* money than without it." To be sure, the availability of financial resources can certainly allay many of life's more pressing problems. At the same time, might it not be the case that a relentless pursuit of success, as measured by financial gain, carries with it a very high opportunity cost? For many people, attainment of the American "way of life" has come with a need to have two breadwinners in the household to realize and to sustain that living standard. Admittedly, many such couples have managed successfully to accommodate the competing demands on their time. For others, however, that has often meant having to give up precious time with ones' family, as well as for leisure activities. At the same time, in a work environment in which earlier paradigms of relative employment security have given way to a growing sense of economic insecurity, the family unit has become subject to greater stress as the grip on the material fruits of success has become more tenuous. As people are forced to work longer hours, and/or to bring their work home with them, meals around the table and quality time with our family often becomes more the exception than the rule. Unable to offer time for and with each other, we offer "things" in place of our time as a tangible symbol of our mutual caring. Having striven for success and attained it, for many the taste of success becomes surprisingly bitter.

Within each of us, I believe, there is present a desire to succeed at whatever we turn our hands to. The desire for success is not intrinsically a bad thing. Rather, when success is defined in narrow economic terms as the attainment of material wealth, and/or the drive for success so defined becomes a compulsion to the exclusion or subordination of other values, happiness or personal satisfaction may remain elusive. It has been said of economists by some that, "they know the price of everything, but the value of nothing." This may be an overly harsh criticism; nonetheless, that admonition reminded me of a quote regarding success attributable to Albert Einstein: "Try not to become a man of success, but rather a man of value." Such advice on the part of this great man was not meant to disparage the yearning to succeed. Rather, Einstein was saying that a life marked by adherence to deeply-held and worthwhile values such as integrity, friendship, loyalty and generosity, among others, is the truest measure of success. In that regard, the inherent wisdom of his words has been reflected over the ages, as for example in the words of Mark in the gospel, *"For what shall it profit a man, if he shall gain the whole world, and lose his soul?"* It should be understood that those who are truly successful are multi-dimensional, and though they may possess material wealth in abundance, it is their character in its entirety and the values they manifest that truly mark them as successful. Thus, in what may be the ultimate paradox, in our preoccupation with attaining success measured in material terms, we may come to the realization that the truest measure of success is, in the main, a life well-lived in which the criteria of that success consist of values that are literally priceless.

I Wish You Enough

AUGUST, 2006

The day started out much like other days. I kissed my wife goodbye, said goodbye to our dog, Sweetpea, and got in the car to drive to work. I put the car in reverse and proceeded to back out of the garage, but after a very short distance the engine died. I turned the key in the ignition again, and despite an insistent cranking, the car refused to start. Numerous repeat operations proved unsuccessful. So, once again this vehicle had failed me, as it had so many times since I had first purchased it. And once again, as I called for a tow truck to take the car to my neighborhood repair shop, I found my mood darkening and my demeanor becoming more and more sullen. "Why me," I thought. Haven't I already contributed enough revenue to the repair shop to have earned a modest financial interest in the operation? How many more things can go wrong, I thought, with this misbegotten example of the decline in America's manufacturing prowess? And, as the promised arrival time for the tow truck came and went, my self-pity and anger seemed to be increasing at an exponential rate.

My wife, who over the long tenure of our marriage has been a fount of tolerance and sage advice, tried to sooth me with her usual good counsel. "It's not worth getting upset over. Whatever it is, we'll get it fixed," she suggested.

"Letting it get to you won't help anything." As I allowed her words to sink in, I recognized the innate wisdom of what she had said. Still, I thought to myself, it *was* a rotten way to start the day, calculating in my mind the likelihood of yet another three-digit repair bill. Surely, I was entitled to indulge myself a bit longer, to seethe awhile, venting my frustration at whatever forces had conspired to ruin my day. Then, after describing the symptoms to the manager of the service station who had long since come to know me on a first-name basis, I proceeded on to my place of work to await word on what the trouble was and what it would cost to be repaired.

It was in this state of mind that I booted up the computer to check on my E-mail messages. And, among them, was one from an old friend with an attachment that bore the subject title, *"I wish you enough!"* I proceeded to read it and felt my residual anger over the earlier morning's events dissipate. At the same time, I found myself increasingly convinced that the text I was reading had not come to me as a matter of mere coincidence. Rather, at a time when I had been preoccupied with lamenting my bad luck, I had been presented by some higher power with an opportunity to put those events in a larger perspective and to do what so many of us fail to do on a regular basis, namely, to reflect upon and to express my gratitude for my overwhelming good fortune.

The attachment concerned a heartfelt departure at an airport security gate between a woman and her elderly mother that was observed and overheard by the writer. As they parted, both mother and daughter expressed the same parting words, "I wish you enough." The observer, her curiosity piqued, approached the elderly mother and inquired, "When you were saying goodbye, I heard you say, 'I wish you enough.' May I ask what that means?" The woman replied that the expression was something that had been handed down from previous generations, including her own parents, who "used to say it to everyone." Then, to explain its meaning more fully, she said, "When we said, 'I wish you enough,' we were wanting the other person to have a life filled with just enough good things to sustain them." As

I reflected on those words, I realized just how meaningful they were, and how often in tallying up the hand that fate has dealt us, we fail to put things in a proper perspective and, as a consequence, we focus disproportionately on those things that try us, rather than on those things that give us joy.

How many of us have had mornings such as the one I experienced? And, more often than not, I suspect that one's reaction to such an experience would be like mine, anger, frustration, and self-pity. Yet, when placed in a broader perspective, the inconvenience of an auto in need of repair should be seen as "a small thing," not worthy of disrupting our emotional equilibrium. In my own case, I left from a comfortable home to go to an office where I am able to practice my craft; I was in good health; I had a caring partner of almost forty-seven years; my dog Sweetpea loved me as well; we had two grown daughters and four beautiful grandchildren; and scores of friends in a city that long has been home to us. To be sure, I realize that what might be an unpleasant event of little real consequence for me, might well be of greater significance to someone else in other circumstances. But, I would contend that the larger truth I had garnered from my car problem and from the serendipitous receipt of the E-mail attachment was still valid. For most of us, if we allow ourselves the luxury of reflection, our lives are filled with far more things that give us joy than try us. In a society in which we have become so accustomed to assigning values in pecuniary terms, we tend to overlook those things we have that are truly priceless. Frequently unable or unwilling to disentangle those things that should give us real pause from those things that, in a larger context, should be of little real concern, we allow ourselves to "stew in a juice of our own making."

So, perhaps the next time a transitory and unpleasant event begins to trigger the "Why me?" response, you might pause to remember the inherent wisdom of a time-tested axiom, "Don't sweat the small stuff!" and ask yourself whether or not, in truth, your life was filled with *more than enough* to sustain you.

In Search of the "Good" Life
JULY, 2006

The world is too much with us; late and soon,
Getting and spending, we lay waste our powers;
Little we see in nature that is ours;
We have given our hearts away, a sordid boon!

—FROM "THE WORLD IS TOO MUCH WITH US,"
BY WILLIAM WORDSWORTH

Quite recently, I came across two seemingly disparate newspaper articles that prompted me to ponder our ongoing quest to attain what we perceive of as the "good" life. One appeared in *The New York Times* and was entitled, *"First Comes the Car; Then the $10,000 License Plate."* It dealt with a Chinese government auction at which individuals were bidding against each other in order to secure a license plate that carried what were perceived to be a favorable set of numbers. The article explained, "For centuries, numbers have served as a second language in China." This preoccupation with numerology coincides with the growing ownership of a new vehicle as the embodiment of having attained the new middle class dream. However, for many aspirants of the good life, the car alone does not suffice. For them, as the article observed, "A license plate has become almost as much of a status symbol as the car." Although the top price for a license plate at this auction was $10,000, the attitude of the bidders might well be summed up in the comments of one bidder who spent $6,750 for his plate:

> "I thought it was rather cheap," said Mr. Ding, a gold chain glinting under his open black sport shirt, "Since I have a nice car, I thought I should get a nice plate."

The second of the two articles appeared in *The Kansas City Star* and was entitled, *"Brookside fixture closes its doors."* It told of the closing of a neighborhood icon, the Dime Store. As the article noted, "The Dime Store earned a sentimental neighborhood status by serving several generations for more than six decades." In an age when the "social" dimension of the shopping experience with small neighborhood establishments has given way to a growing predisposition by American consumers to "shop 'til they drop" at impersonal big box retailers, the Dime Store had become an economic anachronism. The thread that binds these two articles together is that they are both reflective of this age of consumerism where, as the words of Wordsworth suggest, materialism and self-indulgence have become for growing numbers what constitutes the "good" life. It would seem that the accumulation of "things," in societies as different as the Peoples Republic of China and the United States, have become the markers that track our respective ascendancy in our search for the "good" life. Or, might it just be the case that the philosophy of "more is better" that characterizes our infatuation with consumerism is leading us down the wrong path. Rather, might the truth regarding the attainment of the "good" life be found in the musing of the famed architect Mies Van der Rohe, who in commenting on modernity observed, "Less is more."

There can be no doubt that our global community, particularly in the advanced industrial nations of the West, has attained much in the way of material progress. For many, their lives and those of their children have been markedly improved. Per capita income has grown, technology has eased the physical burden of work for many, and longevity has been extended, among other accomplishments. In nations like India and the Peoples Republic of China, a growing middle class is emerging. To be sure, despite huge reservoirs of those who have not yet managed to attain even the lowest rung on the ladder of economic progress in those nations, as well as elsewhere on the planet, the hope for a better future remains fixed on economic growth as the vehicle to create a greater abundance in which more might share. Yet, we are also becoming increasingly cognizant that this progress has not come without growing costs of its own. Insofar as the physical environment is concerned, we are learning anew the old economic aphorism that "there is no free lunch." Those modern technologies and processes that have eased our burdens and increased our inventories of "stuff" have also brought with them environmental degradation and challenges to the carrying capacity and the ability of that same environment to heal itself and to sustain limitless growth at all costs. And, in our personal lives as well, we are finding that the more we have does not necessarily translate into a correspondingly greater sense of well-being and community.

Clearly, we face challenges to our faith in unlimited growth as the "holy grail" in the quest for the "good" life for ourselves and for our less fortunate neighbors on this planet. In an article by Robert Lion in *Le Monde* entitled *"Doing Better with Less,"* the author sounds a clarion call that, "For us, privileged people, the century will be one of sobriety." But, at the same time he asserts that:

"It would be a mistake to see it as a catastrophe: while conceding nothing essential with respect to our way of life, we can consume more cleanly; we can reduce our ecological footprint. ...*Better can be the friend of less.*"

Surely, Lion is right in arguing that "a national public debate is necessary." And in harkening back to the opening words of Wordsworth, Lion is equally correct in admonishing us to:

"stop claiming to dominate nature and the world; let's stop making possession a superior end. Let's put our cherished deviancies, such as the manufacture of desire and its bulimic satisfaction, back in their place. Today's progress must be situated on the side of *being* rather than *having*."

In our search for the "good" life, many have looked outside themselves for the wellspring from which satisfaction emanates. Perhaps what is needed is for us to refocus our vision on within as the source which can lead us to a better and more attainable place. And, in doing so, we may come to the realization that our search begins and ends with us. In that regard, recall the words of T.S. Eliot, taken from his poem *Four Quartets:*

"We shall not cease from exploration
And the end of all our exploring
Will be to arrive where we started
And know the place for the first time."

The Wider Dimensions of Heroism
APRIL, 2006

It would not be altogether inappropriate to regard heroism as something that is associated with extraordinary acts committed either on a field of battle, or under challenging circumstances that would place the actor in a position of danger to one's self. In any case, the hero would undoubtedly be the recipient of public acclaim and would, in all likelihood, be regarded as a role model, someone worthy of emulation.

All of us admire heroes, and can readily cite examples of conduct that warrant being called heroic. Soldiers in combat, first responders such as police and fire personnel, the good Samaritan who stops to pull someone out of a burning automobile at great personal risk, are all examples of individuals whose actions would pass muster under any generally accepted definition of heroism. However, the common denominator of all heroic acts, in addition to the "at risk" environment that must be present, is that the individual's actions must rise above or go beyond that of an observer; he or she must take the initiative to act, and their actions must be extraordinary in nature. Given these constraints that define heroism, it is certainly understandable that acts of heroism would tend to be limited in number, and not likely to be encountered as we go about our lives. However, one might well be able to make a case that the bounds of heroism have been drawn too tightly, and that, if we were to focus more heavily on the hero as an exemplary role model worthy of emulation, detached from the consideration of personal risk to one's life or limb, the order of heroes might be expanded significantly. Perhaps a few examples might be instructive.

In the course of driving to work recently, I listened to a story on National Public Radio that dealt with the subject of caregivers who are themselves seniors. The narrator was speaking of a caregiver who had, for the past ten years or so, ministered to the needs of her younger sister, who had been bed-ridden for all of that time and was in the final stages of Alzheimer's disease. In addition to her sister, under the same roof she was also taking care of her younger brother who had suffered a series of strokes which left him unable to speak, and with greatly limited mobility. Surely, such exertions on behalf of infirm family members would make this caregiver a role model, a "hero" if you will. But, what really added to the legitimacy of such a designation was the fact that the sister was 89 years old; the brother was 94 years old; and, the caregiver was 101 years old. She had chosen the harder path of selfless service to her family, rather than seeing them institutionalized. And, when she was asked why she had made this choice, her response was direct and uncomplicated. She had made a promise to her God that, if she were given the strength to do so, she would spend her remaining years caring for her family members. A promise made was a promise to be kept.

Another example that came to mind involved a man, probably in his 50's or 60's, who I had observed for short periods of time on a number of occasions while I was in my car en route to work. Many of us, I suspect, awake each day with the usual minor aches and pains that elicit a certain amount of self-pity as we go through the regimen of getting ready for our daily schedule. However, more often than not, the aches and pains tend to diminish, and we don't give much thought to the normal physical activities that we engage in going about our business. For the gentleman I observed, however, his physical exertions were anything but normal. For his ability to walk was greatly impaired, and he required a pair of crutches to assist him. Each step required a conscious and exquisitely choreographed act. First, the crutches would be thrust forward and placed a pace or so in front of the man. Then, the left leg was swung outward in an arc that brought that leg alongside the crutch. This same action was then repeated with the right leg and crutch, so that each series of steps were deliberate and measured and his forward progress was painfully slow. I have seen this gentleman "walking" in the rain and snow, in the heat and cold, and on occasion he would have a small dog on a leash as his companion, adding a further burden to his efforts. Yet, his demeanor did not reflect any self-pity at the lot he had drawn. And each time I have seen him, I have reflected on my good fortune to be able to walk without giving that simple act a second thought. His exertions every day seem to me to be the stuff of which heroes are made.

    In these days of intense political partisanship, I am constantly reminded of one of my own personal heroes, Elliott L. Richardson. He was an extraordinary public servant whose common sense, moderation and decency were the attributes that commended him to four different Presidents who appointed him to five different cabinet positions during his tenure in government service. During the Watergate hearings, he was asked by then-President Nixon to fire Archibald Cox, who was serving as the Special Prosecutor investigating the possible involvement of the President in the Watergate break-in. Rather than carrying out an order he felt to be wholly improper, he resigned his position as Attorney General of the United States. His service was not to party, but to the country that he served with such distinction.

    Each of us, I suspect, could readily find role models of our own, who may toil out of any particular limelight, and who may seldom be regarded as genuine heroes. The whistleblower who sees wrongdoing in his/her organization, and comes forward to help bring such activities to the light of day, at considerable risk to their career, is another such example. One might also cite those truly dedicated teachers who spend countless hours before, during, and after class in order to provide their students with the solid grounding and knowledge they will need to succeed in life and to be good citizens. We can all remember such teachers who made a difference in our own lives. And lastly, although many other role models could be cited, we should readily acknowledge perhaps the greatest heroes of all, the many parents who struggle and sacrifice each day to imbue their children with wisdom and character, so that they might better contribute to making our world a better place, and they, in turn, might have a more comfortable life than their parents.

Within the realm of those very "ordinary" people which surrounds us daily, there are undoubtedly everyday heroes of many stripes, whose daily struggles to endure go unnoticed and unacclaimed. That their stories might be told and their exertions might be appreciated is what prompted the author James Agee and his collaborator Walker Evans to write and to photo-illustrate the great work *Let Us Now Praise Famous Men*. For, in truth, their subjects were not at all famous. Indeed, the irony was that they were among the poorest of the poor, living in central Alabama during the depths of the depression and struggling to survive and to maintain their families intact. Yet, it may well be that from among the vast pool of countless and anonymous counterparts in varying circumstances in our society, if we are willing to broaden the dimensions of heroism, we might come across a veritable legion of heroes whose lives should be chronicled and recognized for the noble qualities that are inherent in them.

The Power of "One(s)"
JUNE, 2006

Never doubt that a small group of thoughtful committed individuals can change the world. In fact, it's the only thing that ever has.
—MARGARET MEAD

The recent public announcement by Bill Gates, Chairman of Microsoft, of his intention to step down from his current leadership position served as a reminder of one of those "larger than life" personalities, someone whose efforts have left an indelible mark on our society. Needless to say, we certainly can enumerate other individuals who, over time, have had a profound, positive, and lasting impact on events and on the condition of our world. Surely, it would include individuals in such diverse fields as religion, science, philosophy, politics, and commerce, among others. Whatever the names listed among this coterie of luminaries, surely each of us, on reflection, could flesh out this list with numerous candidates of our own for inclusion into this illustrious pantheon. The common thread that would run through those entries on the list, however, would be the uncommonly large impact they made on their times and on our world. And, while such a list might indeed contain many names, in reality given the overall size of the world's population, that number would be relatively small. Needless to say, for the rest of us, it presumably would be an act of sheer hubris to even think that we too might dwell in such a lofty sphere.

It is undoubtedly not an uncommon feeling these days for each of us to be overcome from time to time with the notion that there is little we can do to alter the flow of the cosmos that sweeps us along in its current. Whatever the particular milieu, this sense of powerlessness often results in a degree of passivity and paralysis that simply reinforces the notion that we really can't change anything even if we should wish to do so. Yet, as noted above, history provides us with numerous examples of individuals who have indeed made a profound difference in their world and in worlds beyond their time. And, we must know intuitively that there are amongst us even now, individuals who by their actions are having an impact on our lives and the lives of generations yet unborn. But what of the rest of us? Although future history might well record the emergence from our ranks of many who will have made a difference, most of us will, in all likelihood, be reconciled to non-celebrity status insofar as our contributions to changing our world are concerned. Yet, might we not be selling ourselves short insofar as our capacity for precipitating changes in the world around us?

A single drop of water may have no perceptible effect when it falls on stone. However, over time the result of innumerable drips on that stone will be to alter its form. Similarly, the weight of a single snowflake is inconsequential. Yet, the collective weight of countless such snowflakes has the power to bring down the structures on which they fall. In the same vein, it is undoubtedly true that the model of the solitary individual with the power single handedly to affect major change is, more often than not, an exaggeration. That is to say, the power of one is most often imperceptible. The power of one(s), of many individuals united in their vision and in their actions, however, is an altogether different situation. All too often, as noted above, we as individuals tend to focus on our individual insignificance as agents of change, compromising the inherent power of our added weight to that of other individuals in concert. How many times when elections take place, have we heard the lament, "What's the point; my vote doesn't count." "I can't change a thing." And yet, have we not seen recently electoral results that turned on just a very few votes in one or another direction.

Those of us who are privileged to live in a democratic society must accept the commensurate responsibility that is levied on each of us to be the stewards of our society and of our planet. We cannot disavow that responsibility by trumpeting our individual powerlessness. In that regard, the words of Mahatma Gandhi are very much to the point: "You must be the change you wish to see in the world." And, from Andy Warhol, the iconic "pop art" painter, we can hear similar sentiments expressed when he noted, "They always say that time changes things, but you actually have to change them yourself."

The nature of most societal change is that it tends to proceed incrementally. Great changes are the exception, rather than the rule. They seldom emerge full-blown, but are the result of a cumulative process over time. And, at the root of all such transformation in our society, as Gandhi observed, there must first be a change in ourselves and in our thinking. Absent such a change at the level of the individual, there can be no effective change at the collective level, thus mitigating the power of the many to continually shape and reshape our world. There resides in each of us the potential to initiate and to contribute to the process of change, if we have the will to seize that potential and to act upon it. If we should fail to participate in that process, or choose to stand aside, we run the risk of living rather barren lives. For, as the futurist Alvin Toffler observed, "Change is not merely necessary to life—it is life." To recognize this reality is to shun the excuse that our power of one, like the drop of water or the single snowflake, is bereft of significance. Rather, in choosing action over inaction, we can make manifest the coda of Margaret Mead and join together as atomistic players in helping to change our world through the combined "power of ones."

What Matters Most?

JUNE, 2007

Without friends no one would choose to live, though he had all other goods.
—ARISTOTLE, NICHOMACHEAN ETHICS

Friendship makes prosperity more brilliant,
and lightens adversity by dividing and sharing it.
—CICERO

Of the many things we may be called upon to do from time to time, perhaps few have the potential to generate as much angst as the act of moving from one place of residence to another. Whether such a move involves a relocation far removed from your former place of residence, or a short distance, the sheer disruption from the norm that it invites offers a jolt to one's sense of order and routine. Particularly when the move entails "downsizing" from a larger place to a smaller one, there is the realization that your accumulated possessions will have to be pared down in order to accommodate the available space in the new dwelling. To this, one should add that the decision of "what matters most" is made even more agonizing when both the volume of those possessions and the attachment to them have grown over a long period of time.

All of these factors were, and still are, in play for my wife and myself as a consequence of our most recent move—the fourteenth—from a large house to a much smaller townhouse just one mile north of our former residence. It should be noted that there is ample storage space in the basement, and we have yet to examine the myriad boxes that await our inspection to determine what to keep and what to dispose of. However, because our primary motivation in moving was to "downsize" and to unburden ourselves of "stuff" we had accumulated from nearly a half century of marriage, we are approaching the task positively. Nonetheless, we have no illusions that in doing so, we will not find ourselves lamenting having to "let go" of numerous things that have held special meaning for us over the years. At the same time, as we assess the value of our attachment to "things," we will, in all likelihood, simultaneously find ourselves determining not only what matters most to us from among our material goods, but also taking the measure of those non-material gifts that have so richly enhanced our lives.

It is no secret that ours is very much a consumption-oriented society. "Shop 'til you drop" regrettably is an apt description for large numbers of avid consumers. Not only does consumption account for two-thirds of the Gross Domestic Product (GDP). At the same time, there seems to be an overwhelming sense that, if "some" of something is good, then "more' of that same thing will undoubtedly be better, a mindset that our conventional economics appears to accept as a given. Thus, for many of us, whatever it is that we have, it seldom seems like "enough." As if our natural inclination to accumulate more material goods weren't sufficiently operative, we are constantly being bombarded by advertisers and marketers to purchase ever "new" and/or "improved" things. So it is that when we are confronted with circumstances that require us to move to another location, we find ourselves in awe at the ever-growing volume of stuff that is to be moved from point

A to point B. And, despite our recognition that surely some of what is to be moved adds little further enhancement to our overall circumstances and ought to be disposed of, our best efforts in that regard often do little to reduce the volume of "things" to which we have become so attached.

As I noted earlier, both my wife and I clearly share some burden of responsibility for having indulged our proclivity for consumption over the years. Having moved many times, one might imagine that, with each move, the process of disposing of superfluous stuff would have made substantial inroads into reducing the amount of material possessions to be moved yet again. However, until the decision was made truly to "downsize," it can hardly have been said that our efforts at "paring down" forced us to take seriously the job of discerning "what mattered most" among our worldly goods. As that process of enlightenment evolves, there is also at work a subtle but insistent impulse to reassess the deeper roots of our happiness, beyond those that may derive from what we own. Increasingly, what has emerged from pursuing the question of what is it that contributes to a truer and more lasting source of happiness or abundance in our lives surprisingly has little to do with our trove of material goods.

Since first moving to Kansas City in 1962, my wife and I have had a number of occasions when we moved away. Still, we always returned to this city we have long called home. Indeed, since 1962, we have come to Kansas City on four separate occasions, the last return coming after a ten-year hiatus as a chaired university Professor in Aurora, Ill. On the occasion of my stepping down from the university into a situation of semi-retirement, I was asked by many associates and colleagues why my wife and I had chosen to return to Kansas City. Quite often, the question would be, "Do you have family there?" And, our response to that query, which required little need for reflection on our part, was always the same. We would say, "No, but we have many dear friends there who seem to us like family."

In point of fact, we have been blessed with the gift of friendship to such an extent that we can truly say that "our cup runneth over." Next to our family, the friends we have made have contributed far more to the abundance in our lives than any material goods we may possess. Perhaps, the 16th century Italian writer and playwright Pietro Aretino said it best, "I keep my friends as misers do their treasure, because of all the things granted us by wisdom, none is greater or better than friendship." Thus, in taking measure of your material good fortune as a contributor in helping to attain happiness, consider the life of Helen Keller. Both deaf and blind, she nonetheless overcame her adversity to live a life that was notable for the profound impact it had in helping others to transcend their adversities. *What mattered most* to her in conferring meaning to her life was summed up in her observation that, "My friends have made the story of my life. In a thousand ways they have turned my limitations into beautiful privileges, and enabled me to walk serene and happy in the shadow cast by my deprivation."

As we may pause on occasion to celebrate our good fortune, let us remember that *what matters most* in accounting for the richness in our lives, more often than not, has less to do with the abundance of our *things,* than with the friends and relationships we have made along the way. For, as expressed in an old Jewish Saying, "Who finds a faithful friend, finds a treasure." May it be so for you.

Reflecting on Retirement

MARCH, 2007

Although I think of myself as an "orderly" person, that self-assessment is often challenged by my wife. In commenting on the various piles of papers on my desk and surrounding workspace, she opined that, no matter how "neat" were those piles, their ongoing and growing presence was indicative of a lack of order. Moved by her criticism, I decided recently to re-examine those stacks in an effort to dispose of those documents that had outlived their utility to me.

As one might suspect, such an exercise does make one question just what on earth motivated you in the first place to consider them worth saving. Thus, a result of my efforts has led to a diminished volume of clutter, surely a worthwhile outcome in and of itself simply in terms of aesthetics. However, a collateral benefit was in finding a profile of a dear friend whom I admire greatly that appeared in a local business publication. For at a point when earlier convention might have dictated he was well past the age of retirement, he remains fully engaged, exhibiting boundless intellectual curiosity and creativity. "What is retirement?" he asked in the article. "If my life is a constant ebb and flow of change and accomplishments and excitement, why should I retire when there's always another hurdle to challenge me?" Now in his upper eighties, and after a lifetime of challenging pursuits in a number of prestigious venues, he holds the position of President of Stowers Innovations Inc., a publishing subsidiary of American Century Investments. Each time I see him, I am continually impressed with his creativity and with the sheer joy he derives from pursuing whatever path those creative urges dictate. Surely our society is enriched in having such a person remain active and involved, rather than "put out to pasture."

There would appear to be something inherently counter-intuitive about the concept of retirement as we have known it. After having spent a lifetime garnering skills that make one more productive and more valuable either to an employer or in self-employment, there is an expectation that on reaching a specific age—65 years in most instances—one should step down from a work regimen, taking with you the accumulated skills and the work ethic that imparted value to your efforts. In its place, presumably, a life of leisure awaits you as you enjoy your remaining days, if you are fortunate enough to have the financial wherewithal to sustain you in retirement. For those who are in such a position and of such disposition, retirement may indeed be the appropriate decision and the reward for a lifetime of hard work. At the same time, for increasing numbers of potential retirees, an inability to have adequate resources to accommodate a life of leisure has forced them to avoid retirement from their current positions, if possible, or to seek alternate employment when they are forced to step down from the jobs they formerly held. Thus, we might sort people of retirement age into two camps; those who choose to retire and can afford to do so, and those who would like to retire, but find themselves financially unable to do so. But, what of people such as my friend in the article? He falls into neither category, and I suspect that there are a substantial number of individuals like him who have chosen not to retire, even though they are in a position to do so comfortably.

Several factors suggest that this cohort might be sizable and growing. A huge number of post-World War II "baby boomers" is approaching retirement age. Advancing technology has helped to lift many of the more demanding physical tasks associated with "blue collar" jobs from the shoulders of our nation's manufacturing workers. In addition, the nature of work in our economy has shifted toward the services sector and away from manufacturing. Thus, more workers are approaching retirement age with far fewer physical limitations that would render them either unable to work further, or unwilling to extend their work regimen. At the same time, advances in health care and medical technology continue to extend our longevity so that more and more individuals are physically fit to work for years well beyond the traditional age of retirement, a fact recognized by the Social Security Administration. Such a pool of individuals, with both the skills and the desire to remain productive, may represent a heretofore unappreciated and obscured source of "competitive advantage" for our economy. At a time when global outsourcing of jobs has called into question our nation's ability to continue to sustain a vibrant and secure middle class, there exists a potential reserve army of either unutilized or underutilized seniors both ready and willing to bring their talents to bear in helping to resuscitate the proud label that reads "Made in America." And, for those who no longer wish to continue in the conventional job market, surely our society can offer them a wide range of opportunities to pursue much-needed and personally rewarding volunteer or public service work.

How many of us have seen examples of individuals who, while quite capable of further work effort, nonetheless chose to retire? In many instances, as noted earlier, that decision to retire provided the retiree with a long-sought and well-deserved opportunity to pursue a fruitful and happy change from hewing to the rigors of a regular work schedule. My own father could have been a "poster boy" for just such an outcome. At the same time, can we not also remember those instances in which someone we knew, or heard of, chose to retire only to find that retirement stripped from them the exhilaration and camaraderie associated with a work environment that had resonated with constant challenges and opportunities to put their skills to good uses? For some, the relish with which retirement was anticipated becomes replaced with a bitter taste of disappointment or disillusionment as inactivity takes its toll from both their physical and emotional wellbeing. Although I am a senior citizen chronologically, like my friend I consider myself extremely fortunate to have refrained from taking formal retirement in favor of "staying in the game," describing my situation as "semi-retirement" in an intellectually stimulating work environment that affords me an ongoing opportunity to do interesting things. I am equally sure that my bride of some 47+ years also approves of that decision, for I would surely not wish on that good person the burden of my company "24/7."

In the article profiling my friend, there is included a quote from him that that I would offer to anyone nearing the retirement threshold: "The way the pendulum goes back and forth, what you thought was the end of something, it really could be the beginning of something else." It is a thought well worth keeping in mind in the event, one day, you should find yourself reflecting on retirement.